First World War
and Army of Occupation
War Diary
France, Belgium and Germany

9 DIVISION
2 Lowland Brigades
Headquarters
1 April 1919 - 6 November 1919

WO95/1776/6

The Naval & Military Press Ltd
www.nmarchive.com
Published in association with The National Archives

Published by

The Naval & Military Press Ltd

Unit 10 Ridgewood Industrial Park,

Uckfield, East Sussex,

TN22 5QE England

Tel: +44 (0) 1825 749494

www.naval-military-press.com

www.nmarchive.com

This diary has been reprinted in facsimile from the original. Any imperfections are inevitably reproduced and the quality may fall short of modern type and cartographic standards.

© **Crown Copyright**
Images reproduced by permission of The National Archives, London, England, 2015.

Contents

Document type	Place/Title	Date From	Date To
Heading	Lowland (9th) Division HQ 2nd Lowland Bde 1919 Apr-1919 Nov Disbanded		
War Diary	Villa Kortenbach	01/04/1919	01/04/1919
War Diary	89 Weyer Ohligs	02/04/1919	02/04/1919
War Diary	Rhineland Germany	03/04/1919	30/04/1919
Operation(al) Order(s)	2nd Lowland Brigade Order No.1	05/04/1919	05/04/1919
Miscellaneous	Action Of Brigade In Event Of Civil Disturbances	12/04/1919	12/04/1919
Miscellaneous	5/5th Royal Scots	23/04/1919	23/04/1919
Miscellaneous	2nd Lowland Brigade Reinforcements For April 1919		
Miscellaneous	Lowland Division	04/06/1919	04/06/1919
War Diary	Villa Kortenbach	01/05/1919	01/05/1919
War Diary	89 Weyer Ohligs	02/05/1919	02/05/1919
War Diary	Rhineland Germany	03/05/1919	31/05/1919
Operation(al) Order(s)	2nd Lowland Brigade Order No.2	26/05/1919	26/05/1919
Miscellaneous	Table "A"		
Miscellaneous	2nd Lowland Brigade May 1919 Reinforcements		
Miscellaneous	Table "B" To Accompany 2nd Lowland Brigade Order No.2	27/05/1919	27/05/1919
Miscellaneous	Amendment No.1 To 2nd Lowland Brigade Order No.2		
Miscellaneous	Addendum No.2 To 2nd Lowland Brigade Order No.2	26/05/1919	26/05/1919
War Diary	Villa Kortenbach	02/06/1919	02/06/1919
War Diary	89 Weyer Ohligs	12/06/1919	12/06/1919
War Diary	Rhineland Germany	14/06/1919	25/06/1919
War Diary	Villa Kortenbach	27/06/1919	27/06/1919
War Diary	89 Weyer Ohligs	28/06/1919	28/06/1919
War Diary	Rhineland Germany	30/06/1919	30/06/1919
Miscellaneous	Amendment To 2nd Lowland Brigade Order No.5	27/06/1919	27/06/1919
Operation(al) Order(s)	2nd Lowland Brigade Order No.5	25/06/1919	25/06/1919
Operation(al) Order(s)	2nd Lowland Brigade Order No.4		
Operation(al) Order(s)	2nd Lowland Brigade Order No.3	19/06/1919	19/06/1919
Miscellaneous	Table "C"		
Miscellaneous	To All Recipients Of 2nd Lowland Brigade Order No.2 dated 26/5/19	26/05/1919	26/05/1919
Miscellaneous	Addendum No.4 To 2nd Lowland Brigade Order No.2 dated 26/5/19	26/05/1919	26/05/1919
Miscellaneous	Addendum No.3 To 2nd Lowland Brigade Order No.2 Dated 26/5/19	26/05/1919	26/05/1919
Miscellaneous	Amendment No.3 To 2nd Lowland Brigade Order No.2 Dated 26/5/19	26/05/1919	26/05/1919
Miscellaneous	All Recipients of 2nd Lowland Brigade Order No.2 dated 26/5/19	26/05/1919	26/05/1919
Miscellaneous	Amendment No.2 To 2nd Lowland Brigade Order No.2 Dated 26th May 1919	26/05/1919	26/05/1919
Miscellaneous	Table "A"		
Miscellaneous	B.M.18 Lowland Division	04/08/1919	04/08/1919
Miscellaneous	Reinforcements		
War Diary	Gill Rhineland Germany Sheet 3 R N.W. 1.25000 N 6704	03/07/1919	30/07/1919
Operation(al) Order(s)	2nd Lowland Brigade Order No.6	07/07/1919	07/07/1919
Miscellaneous	Addendum No.1 To 2nd Lowland Brigade Order No.6	08/07/1919	08/07/1919

Type	Description	Start	End
Miscellaneous	B.M.3/1 Lowland Division 'A'	04/09/1919	04/09/1919
Miscellaneous	Reinforcements		
War Diary	7 Holy Strasse	07/08/1919	07/08/1919
War Diary	Duren	07/08/1919	07/08/1919
War Diary	Rhineland Germany	12/08/1919	29/08/1919
Operation(al) Order(s)	2nd Lowland Brigade Order No.7	13/08/1919	13/08/1919
Miscellaneous	Table A To Accompany 2nd Lowland Brigade Order No.7		
Miscellaneous	2nd Lowland Brigade Reinforcements		
War Diary	7 Holy Strasse	15/09/1919	15/09/1919
War Diary	Duren	15/09/1919	15/09/1919
War Diary	Rhineland Germany	17/09/1919	30/09/1919
Miscellaneous	2nd Lowland Brigade Operation Order No.10	03/11/1919	03/11/1919
War Diary	Duren	01/10/1919	31/10/1919
Miscellaneous	B.M./8/ D.S.	30/10/1919	30/10/1919
Miscellaneous	2nd Lowland Brigade Defence Scheme		
Miscellaneous	Defence Scheme For Civil Disturbances Duren Officer In Command O.C 11th Royal Scots Hindenburg Barracks		
Miscellaneous	Appendix 1		
Miscellaneous	Defence Scheme For Civil Disturbances		
Miscellaneous	Appendix "B"		
Miscellaneous	Defence Scheme For Civil Disturbance-Elsdorf Area		
Miscellaneous	BM/5/D.S	18/10/1919	18/10/1919
Miscellaneous	Duren Defence Scheme	18/10/1919	18/10/1919
Miscellaneous	Localities To Be Defended		
Miscellaneous	Signal for Alarming the Town		
War Diary	Duren	01/11/1919	06/11/1919
Operation(al) Order(s)	2nd Lowland Brigade Order No.9		
Miscellaneous	2nd Lowland Brigade Order No.9		

LOWLAND (9th) DIVISION

HQ 2nd LOWLAND BDE

1919 APR — 1919 NOV.

DISBANDED

WAR DIARY for April 1919. Army Form C. 2118.

HQ 2 Portland Infy Bgd

INTELLIGENCE SUMMARY.

(Erase heading not required.)

Place	Date	Hour	Summary of Events and Information	Remarks and references to Appendices
VILLA KORTENBACH 89 WEYER 2.4.F.19 O.H.L.G.S. RHINELAND. 3.4.19 GERMANY.	1.4.19		Training and Education.	
	2.4.19		— do —	
	3.4.19		The Cadre of 12th Bn. Royal Scots left to-day for England.	
-do-	4.4.19		Training and Education.	
-do-	5.4.19		Training and Education. Bde. Order No.1 issued to all concerned for move of 6th, 10th SB on 6th and 7th April to WALD from MULHEIM, and to take over 1 post from 11th Royal Scots and 5½/6 Royal Scots on 8th April.	Apr. 1.
-do-	6.4.19		Sunday	
-do-	7.4.19		Capt. C.N. RYAN DSO m.c., Royal Engineers assumed duties of Brigade Major, vice Capt. R.N. DUKE DSO m.c., proceeding to England for demobilization.	
	8.4.19			

WAR DIARY
or
INTELLIGENCE SUMMARY.

Army Form C. 2118.

Place	Date	Hour	Summary of Events and Information	Remarks and references to Appendices
۔	8.4.19		Training and Education. Lieut W.G. SINCLAIR 11th Royal Scots assumed duties of Staff Capt, Civil Administration, vice Capt. C.C.	
WINCHESTER mlc. to duty with 1st Bn Royal Scots				
۔	9.4.19		Training and Education	
۔	10.4.19		Do. Do. A Conference of Commanding Officers was held at Brigade H.Q. at 13.00 hours.	
	11.4.19		Training and Education. The Brigade Major attended a Conference of Brigade Majors and Adjutants at the Divisional College at 3 p.m.	
	12.4.19		Training and Education. BRS/14 issued to all concerned regarding "Action of the Brigade in Event of Civil disturbances"	APP.2.
	13.4.19		Sunday.	

Army Form C. 2118.

WAR DIARY
or
INTELLIGENCE SUMMARY.
(Erase heading not required.)

Instructions regarding War Diaries and Intelligence Summaries are contained in F. S. Regs., Part II. and the Staff Manual respectively. Title pages will be prepared in manuscript.

Place	Date	Hour	Summary of Events and Information	Remarks and references to Appendices
-D-	14.4.19		Training and Education	
-D-	15.4.19		-do-	
-D-	16.4.19		-do-	
-D-	17.4.19		-do-	
-D-	18.4.19		(Good Friday) Observed as a holiday.	
-D-	19.4.19		Training and Education. General Sir Wm. ROBERTSON, G-in-C, British Army of the Rhine, visited the Brigade area.	
-D-	20.4.19		Sunday.	
-D-	21.4.19		The Brigade School was opened to-day at HAAN each Battn sending 4 young Officers and 12 N.C.Os. to the first course. Each course would cover a period of 4 or 6 weeks.	
-D-	22.4.19		Training and Education.	
-D-	23.4.19		-do-	

Army Form C. 2118.

WAR DIARY
or
INTELLIGENCE SUMMARY.
(Erase heading not required.)

Instructions regarding War Diaries and Intelligence Summaries are contained in F. S. Regs., Part II. and the Staff Manual respectively. Title pages will be prepared in manuscript.

Place	Date	Hour	Summary of Events and Information	Remarks and references to Appendices
-D-	23.4.19 (contd)		Bro/4/5/3 issued to all concerned for move of 5th/6th Royal Scots to OM.I.C.S on 28th April.	App. 3.
-D-	24.4.19.		Training and Education. The Brigadier inspected the 56th Royal Scots during the forenoon. The Brigade Major and Staff Capt. attended a Conference at Divisional College at 3.15 p.m. 2nd Lowland Reynold Defence Scheme issued to all concerned, cancelling Appendix 2.	Appendix 2.
-D-	25.4.19			
-D-	26.4.19.		Training and Education.	
	27.4.19/		The Brigade Commander attended a Conference at Division H.Q. at 10.15 a.m., to discuss details of a probable further advance into Germany owing to the political situation.	

WAR DIARY
or
INTELLIGENCE SUMMARY.

Army Form C. 2118.

Place	Date	Hour	Summary of Events and Information	Remarks and references to Appendices
D¹	27.4.19		A conference of Commanding Officers was held at Bde. HQ. at 10 a.m. to discuss details of the probable advance into Germany.	
	28.4.19		Training and Education. A course under the Divisional General Staff, began at WALD. A Corps School was commenced to-day for a period of two days. The following are attending the course :— 2 Adjutants and 1 officer per Company from each Infantry Bn. 1 Senior and 1 Junior N.C.O. per Company from each Infantry Bn.	
	29.4.19			
	30.4.19		Training and Education.	

Army Form C. 2118.

WAR DIARY
or
INTELLIGENCE SUMMARY.

(Erase heading not required.)

Instructions regarding War Diaries and Intelligence Summaries are contained in F. S. Regs., Part II. and the Staff Manual respectively. Title pages will be prepared in manuscript.

Place	Date	Hour	Summary of Events and Information	Remarks and references to Appendices
D-	30.4.19		Training and Education.	
			Reinforcements -------------	App. A.

Anderson
Brigade Major
2nd Canadian Brigade

APP. 1. War Diary

SECRET.   2nd Lowland Brigade Order No. 1.   Copy No. 11

1. On 6th and 7th April the 6th K.O.S.B. at MULHEIM will be relieved by the 16th H.L.I. (Pioneers), and will return to their former billets in the western part of WALD.

2. The relief will be carried out as follows :-

   (a) On 6th April 16th H.L.I. (less 2 Coys.) move by train leaving SOLINGEN about 09.00 to MULHEIM in relief of 2 Coys. 6th K.O.S.B. After relief 2 Coys., 6th K.O.S.B. move to OHLIGS by train leaving MULHEIM about 17.00, and march thence to billets in WALD.

   (b) On 7th April 2 Coys., 16th H.L.I. move by train leaving SOLINGEN about 09.00 to MULHEIM in relief of 6th K.O.S.B. (less 2 Coys.). After relief 6th K.O.S.B. (less 2 Coys.) move to OHLIGS by train leaving MULHEIM about 17.00, and march thence to billets in WALD.

   (c) Train accommodation has been requested on each day for 12 officers and 300 O.Rs.

   (d) Transport will move by road on each day.

3. To increase accommodation in WALD, 5th/6th Royal Scots will move two Companies not at present undergoing training to billets at GRAFRATH. These Companies will be clear of billets in WALD by 17.00 on 6th April.

4. Billeting party from 6th K.O.S.B. will be sent to take over old billets in WALD on the morning of the 6th April.

5. Lieut. HEDDLE, M.O., 16th H.L.I., will report to 6th K.O.S.B. at MULHEIM to-day, 5th April, to arrange details of relief of guards on 6th and 7th April.

6. Further instructions, train times, etc., will be notified later.

7. (a) On 8th April 6th K.O.S.B. will take over the present Left (No.3) Examining Post of 5th/6th Royal Scots, and the present Right (No.1) Post of 11th Royal Scots.

   (b) Details of this relief will be arranged between Commanding Officers concerned.

   (c) On completion of this relief the Posts on the Brigade/

- 2 -

Brigade front will be renumbered as under :-

New No. of Post.	Map Reference of Post.	To be found by.
1.	A.31.05, ELBERFELD 1/25,000 Sheet)	
2.	A.36.14.(KLUSE), -do.- -do.-)	5/6th R.Scots.
3.	A.28.09. -do.- -do.-)	
4.	A.12.09. -do.- -do.-)	6th K.O.S.B.
5.	E.94.08. -do.- -do.-)	
6.	E.88.06. -do.- -do.-)	11th R.Scots.
7.	K.37.83. DUSSELDORF 1/25,000 Sh.)	

The necessary alterations on all maps, order boards at posts, etc. will be made forthwith.

8. Completion of all moves and reliefs detailed in this Order will be reported by wire to Brigade H.Q. by all units concerned.

9. A C K N O W L E D G E.

Issued at _____ 5/4/19.

Captain,
Brigade Major.

Copy No. 1 to 5th/6th Royal Scots.
        2 to 11th Royal Scots.
        3 to 6th K. O. S. B.
        4 to 90th Field Coy., R.E.
        5 to 27th Field Ambulance.
        6 to 106th Coy., R.A.S.C.
        7 to 16th H.L.I. (Pioneers).
        8 to Lowland Division.
        9 to   -do.-
        10 and 11 to War Diary.
        12 to 14. File.

App. 2

SECRET.

B.M./4.
12th April, 1919.

ACTION OF BRIGADE
IN EVENT
OF CIVIL DISTURBANCES.

Refs - DUSSELDORF)
SOLINGEN) 1/25,000.
ELBERFELD)

1. The following instructions for action in the case of civilian disturbances are to be regarded as provisional and are based on some preliminary instructions received from the Division.
   Final instructions under this heading and also for certain other eventualities will be issued in due course when they are finally approved.

2. The duty of the Brigade within its present Sub-Area is primarily to maintain law and order, and enforce the regulations laid down for the Occupied Territory.

3. As far as the Sub Area is concerned the main centres of probable disturbances may be taken as WALD, HAAN and OHLIGS, but plans must be thought out to meet an armed mob entering the Sub-Area from either SOLINGEN, ELBERFELD or DUSSELDORF.

4. (a). In order to be prepared to deal with disturbances of this nature, every unit in the Sub-Area will detail daily 25% of its strength as an Inlying Picquet. In the case of battalions of the Brigade this will consist of one of the companies not employed on the Post Line.
   The Inlying Picquet will not remain under arms but must be capable of turning out, fully armed and equipped, at very short notice at any time of the day or night.
   Ammunition in the proportion of a 120 rounds per man will be held in readiness for issue.

   (b). In addition not more than 10% at one time of the remainder of a unit, exclusive of organised parties away on leave, on river trips, etc., will be allowed a pass outside the Sub-Area.

5. (a). The signal for the return to billets of all men in the Sub-Area, or outside it, if they hear the signal, will be a series of three short blasts given on certain selected factory hooters and a series of three tolls sounded on certain church bells.

   (b)./

- 2 -

(b). Each battalion will select one factory and one
church in their area at which this signal can be given
in case of alarm, and will report to Brigade H.Q.
their positions and the arrangements made for
having the Signal sounded when required.

(c). This signal is uniform throughout the whole
Divisional Area, and in the event of it being started
in any Sub-Area it will at once be taken up
throughout all four Sub-Areas.

(d). All ranks must be made to understand quite
clearly that when they hear this signal they must
return at once as quickly as possible to their
billets.

6. (a). When the alarm has been given subsequent
action by troops in the sub-area will be carried out
in two phases:-

(i) Concentration at Alarm Posts.
(ii) Move to certain selected localities
previously decided upon.

(b). Units will order the first phase automatically
on the alarm signal and are authorised to order
the second phase, if the situation demands it,
before the receipt of orders from the Brigade,
reporting their action to Brigade H.Q. at once.

7. Units located in the Sub-Area will be responsible for
the following areas and will select the necessary alarm
posts

5/6th Royal Scots.	GRAFRATH. CENTRAL. WALD, E. of an N. and S. line through the Church at F.17.central.
11th Royal Scots.	HAAN.
6th K.O.S.B.	WALD, W. of an N. and S. line through the Church at F.17.central.
90th Field Coy R.E.) 1 Bty. 51st Bde. R.F.A. 'B' Coy. Lowland M-G. Bn.	VICTORIA STRASSE Cross Roads at F.37.65. MERSCHEID. Northern exits to SOLINGEN.
51st Bde. R.F.A. (less 1 Bty).	WEYER

OHLIGS must be dealt with by troops billetted in that
area, till other troops can be moved in.

8/

- 3 -

8. During the concentration the following preliminary steps will be taken :-

   (a). Existing guards will be doubled.

   (b). Guards will be posted over dumps of arms and ammunition, telephone exchanges (with a view to protecting the interior of the exchange and not the lines leading to it), Power Stations and Banks.
   Important avenues of movement such as squares, main thoroughfares and open spaces in towns will be commanded by Lewis and Vickers guns(e.g. from the windows of houses).

   (c). Burgomasters and other convenient influential civilian personages will be seized and held as hostages.

   (d). All transport will be loaded and ready to hook in.

   (e). All parties moving about will be as strong as possible to reduce the risk of being overpowered.

   (f). Runners will move in pairs.

   (g). All movement through streets occupied by enemy snipers will be along the right hand side of the road.

9. (a). Only the minimum number of troops absolutely necessary for the above guard duties, etc. should be employed, so that as strong a body as possible may be available as a mobile reserve.

   (b). A report will be sent to Brigade H.Q. stating the number of troops still left on hand available for general purposes.

10. (a). As regards the occupation of selected localities to deal with armed risings within the Brigade area, the general principle will be to isolate the rioters and prevent them spreading to neighbouring towns.

    (b). With this object in view Battalion Commanders will reconnoitre at once the best positions to occupy as follows :-

    5/6th Royal Scots.   Highground East of WALD in Squares F.38 & 48 and South of GRAFRATH in Squares F. 39 & 49, also the village of CENTRAL.

    11th Royal Scots/

11th Royal Scots.   High ground at the Southern and
                    Eastern outskirts of HAAN in
                    squares K.97 & 98 and F.O.8.

6th K.O.S.B.   The high ground at the S.W.
                    end of WALD on the VICTORIA STR.
                    It must also be prepared to detail
                    one company to deal with OHLIGS.
                    This battalion would be regarded
                    as the Brigade Reserve.

(c). The 51st Brigade R.F.A. and 'B' Coy. Lowland
M.G. Battalion will reconnoitre forthwith and be
prepared to take up positions from which they can
command the exits and main streets in HAAN, WALD,
GRAFRATH and OHLIGS.

11. (a). In the event of disturbances occurring outside the
Sub-Area, e.g. from ELBERFELD, SOLINGEN or
DUSSELDORF and threatening to enter the Sub-Area
(vide para. 3) it may be necessary to occupy certain
positions or to assume positions of readiness —
which briefly stated are :-

(i) <u>Against an invasion from ELBERFELD via
VOHWINKEL and GRAFRATH.</u>
The high ground N. and W. of GRAFRATH on the
line KLUSE - HOLTHAUSEN (squares A.31 ± A.0.0.).
The best defensive line in the vicinity is
approximately along the perimeter from KLUSE
to the Post at A.12.09. and thence to the high
ground at HOLTHAUSEN.   This gives a commanding
position from which the approaches from VOHWINKEL
and GRUITEN can be commanded.
Distribution of units - 5/6th Royal Scots on
the Right ' 11th Royal Scots on the left - Inter
Battalion boundary track at A.21.10 - BOLTHAUSEN -
BUXHAUS inclusive to 5/6th Royal Scots ' 6th
K.O.S.B. in Brigade Reserve.

(ii) <u>Against an Invasion from SOLINGEN.</u>
The high ground on the approximate line of
the road WALD - KETSBERG from which all approaches
from SOLINGEN can be dominated.   The high ground
about Squares F.48 and F.27. command these
approaches.
Distribution of Units - 5/6th Royal Scots
occupying the line as above.   Remainder of
Brigade in a position of readiness in its
respective areas.

(iii) (a). <u>Against an invasion from DUSSELDORF.</u>
The 2nd Infantry Brigade would in the
first instance be held in readiness to
support the 3rd Infantry Brigade -
preliminary move 6th K.O.S.B. to OHLIGS.
(b). <u>Against an invasion from DUSSELDORF
developing from MILLRATH and the N.W.</u>
The wired position along the general line
covering HAAN ' HILL 107 ± HILDEN.
Distribution/

Distribution of units - 11th Royal Scots on the Right - 6th K.O.S.B. on the left - Inter Battalion boundary track through cross roads at K.66.72 inclusive to 11th Royal Scots - 5/6th Royal Scots in Brigade Reserve.

(b). The 51st Brigade R.F.A. and 'B' Coy. Lowland Battalion M.G.C. will be prepared to move to suitable positions to support the infantry in any of the cases referred to above. The necessary reconnaissance of positions and routes of approach will be carried out forthwith.

12. COMMUNICATIONS.

In all cases of civil disturbances disaffection amongst the inhabitants would probably result at once in the breakdown of the telephone system.

Reliance therefore must be placed on other means of communication.

The Brigade Signal Officer will consult Commanding Officers as to the probable position of their command posts in all the cases considered above and will draw up a scheme of signalling by visual and other means between them and Brigade H.Q., and also between Brigade H.Q. and Division H.Q. and Flanking Brigade H.Q.

The following points between which visual signalling is possible may prove useful :-

```
        K.97.95 to F.11.71.
                   F.05.85.
                   F.08.94.
                   A.45.08.
                   K.82.96.
        F.08.94. to F.05.85.
                    F.24.85.
                    F.11.71.
```

(sgd) C.R. Ryan
Captain,
Brigade Major.
2nd Lowland Brigade.

Copies to :-

5/6th Royal Scots.	106th Coy A.S.C.
11th Royal Scots.	27th Field Amb.
6th K.O.S.B.	1st Lowland Brigade.
51st Brigade R.F.A.	3rd Lowland Brigade.
90th Field Coy R.E.	Lowland Division 'G'.
Lowland Bn. M.G.C.	Lowland Division 'Q'.
'B' Coy. Lowland Bn. M.G.C.	Office.

App. 3

BM 3/2.
23rd April, 1919.

5/6th Royal Scots.
11th Royal Scots.
6th K.O.S.B.

1. (a) The 5/6th Royal Scots will move from WALD to OCHAUS on
       Monday 28th inst.
   (b) Detailed instructions regarding billets have been issued
       by the Staff Captain.
   (c) Billets in WALD must be cleared by noon. No restrictions as
       to route.

2. The 6th K.O.S.B. will hand over No. 4 Post (GHEYN)
   to the 11th Royal Scots, and will take over No. 1 Post (JLUSE)
   and No. 2 Post (HOHN) from the 5/6th Royal Scots under
   arrangements to be made by Battalion Commanders concerned.

   Reliefs to be complete by midnight Saturday, 26th inst.,
   and completion to be reported to this office.

3. Please acknowledge.

                                        Captain,
                                        Brigade Major,
                                        2nd Lowland Brigade.

Copies to :- Division 'G'.   20th Fd. Coy. R.E.
              "   'Q'.   27th Fd. Ambulance.
              D.A.P.M.   105th Coy. R.A.S.C.
              Staff Captain.   51st Bde. R.F.A.
              Brigade Signal Officer.
              Brigade Education Officer.
              Staff Captain, Civil Administration.

App.4

2nd LOWLAND BRIGADE.

REINFORCEMENTS FOR APRIL, 1919.

	Officers.	Other Ranks.
5/6th Royal Scots.	11	275.
11th Royal Scots.	13	181.
6th K. O. S. B.	8	90.
Total.	32	546

B.M./5/2.
4th June, 1919.

Lowland Division.

Herewith War Diaries of Brigade Headquarters and 3 Battalions of this Brigade for May, 1919.

Please acknowledge.

C. Anderson Lt.
Brigadier-General,
Commanding 2nd Lowland Brigade.

Army Form C. 2118.

WAR DIARY for May, 1919.
INTELLIGENCE SUMMARY
(Erase heading not required).

Instructions regarding War Diaries and Intelligence Summaries are contained in F. S. Regs. Part II. and the Staff Manual respectively. Title pages will be prepared in manuscript.

Place	Date	Hour	Summary of Events and Information	Remarks and references to Appendices
Villa	1.5.19		Training and Education	
KORTENBACH	2.5.19		Meeting of Div Sports Officers and Brigade Major at Rgt to adjust at 1500 hours	
OPWEIER				
OHLIGS	3.5.19		Brigade Commander inspected an L.J. lumber from and Battalion lined with T Gate	
RHINELAND	4.5.19		Sunday	
GERMANY	5.5.19		Training & Education	
	6.5.19		- Do -	
	7.5.19		- Do -	
	8.5.19		H.R.H. the Duke of Connaught visited HEAN Training and Education Conference of Sports Officers at Divisional College	
	9.5.19		Training and Education	
	10.5.19		- Do - Instructions issued to support Battalion to deploy T shaped strata at permitted posts on 12 & May from 0930 till 1330 hours in order to provide practice for squadron of 47 squadron R.A.F.	
	11.5.19		Sunday	

Army Form C. 2118.

WAR DIARY for May 1919
or
INTELLIGENCE SUMMARY.
(Erase heading not required.)

Instructions regarding War Diaries and Intelligence Summaries are contained in F. S. Regs., Part II. and the Staff Manual respectively. Title page will be prepared in manuscript.

Place	Date	Hour	Summary of Events and Information	Remarks and references to Appendices
-Do-	12.5.19		Training and Education. Conference of Brigade Commanders / Divl. Commander at Brigade H.Q. at 15.30 hrs	
-Do-	13.5.19		Training and Education. Conference of Battalion Commanders at Brigade H.Q at 14.30 hours	
-Do-	14.5.19		Training and Education	
-Do-	15.5.19		-Do-	
-Do-	16.5.19		-Do-	
-Do-	17.5.19		-Do-	
-Do-	18.5.19		Sunday. Conference of Brigade Commanders at Divl Commanders Headquarters at 10.30 hrs	
-Do-	19.5.19		Conference of Battalion Commanders at Brigade H.Q. at 14.30	
-Do-	20.5.19		Training and Education. 1st Course at Brigade School terminated.	
-Do-	21.5.19		Training and Education. Conference of Brigade Commanders	
-Do-	22.5.19		Training and Education	
-Do-	23.5.19		Conference of Battalion Commanders at Brigade H.Q. at 10.00 hrs	

Army Form C. 2118.

WAR DIARY for May 1919
or
INTELLIGENCE SUMMARY
(Erase heading not required.)

Instructions regarding War Diaries and Intelligence Summaries are contained in F. S. Regs., Part II. and the Staff Manual respectively. Title pages will be prepared in manuscript.

Place	Date	Hour	Summary of Events and Information	Remarks and references to Appendices
Do	24.5.19		Training and Education	
Do	25.5.19		Sunday	
Do	26.5.19		2nd Course at Brigade School assembled. Training and 2 lectures. Tatoho displayed again at parade first as notes in 10th May who displayed again to all internees mine. 2nd Koarhant Brigade orders No 2 issued to all internees mine found in event of repeating domestic being terminated	APP 1
Do	27.5.19		Training and 2 lectures. Conference at Brigade Headquarters at 1430 hrs Instructions issued to 5/6 Royal Scots to send a Company to 3rd Royal Scots in care of detachments due to strikes. Brigade area Conrurt in care of detachments due to strikes.	
Do	28.5.19		Training and 2 lectures. 1 Coy 5/6 Royal Scots moved to Bonnett in accordance with above instructions	
Do	29.5.19		Q Branch Commander visited Battalion inspected billets etc and interviewed officers	
Do	30.5.19		Training and Education	
Do	31.5.19		No Reinforcements	

Army Form C. 2118.

WAR DIARY
INTELLIGENCE SUMMARY
(Erase heading not required.)

Instructions regarding War Diaries and Intelligence Summaries are contained in F. S. Regs., Part II. and the Staff Manual respectively. Title pages will be prepared in manuscript.

Place	Date	Hour	Summary of Events and Information	Remarks and references to Appendices
D.O.	20		Reinforcements	APP 2
			Chuwont for Captain, Reg major 2nd Gurkha Rif.	
	4.5.19.			

A 5834 Wt. W4973/M687 750,000 8/16 B. D. & L. Ltd. Forms/C.2118/13.

SECRET.

War Diary   APP. 1

2nd LOWLAND BRIGADE ORDER No. 2.   26/5/19.

Ref. 1 : 200,000 COLN (Sheet 59).
    "   "   MUNSTER (Sheet 55).

Special Maps A (COLN $\frac{1}{200,000}$ Sheet 59))
              B (METTMANN 1/25,000, Sheet 2rN.E.) Attached.
              and ELBERFELD 1/25,000 Sheet 2.s.N.W.))

---

1. (a) In the event of the existing Armistice being terminated, hostilities will recommence, after 72 hours warning to the enemy, on a day to be known as J day.

   (b) The Allies will then advance to seize the RUHR BASIN, the German railways essential for an advance, together with all rolling stock and German personnel for working the lines under our orders.

   (c) The exact time and date of the advance will be notified later.

2.   The general lines on which the advance will be carried out will be as follows :-

   (a) On "J" day the II Corps will advance to the general line REMSCHEID - BARMEN - WULFRATH (exclusive) - METTMANN - DUSSELDORF.

        The IV Corps will move forward and take over the present II Corps area, the Highland Division taking over the present area of the Lowland Division.

   (b) On "J plus 1" day portions of the VI Corps will pass through the II Corps and continue the advance. Portions of the Southern Division (II Corps) will pass through the Lowland Division, which will not move.

        In addition the Belgian forces will cross the RHINE and advance in a north easterly direction with the DUSSELDORF-METTMANN-WULFRATH-LANGENBG-HATTINGEN-WITTEN-HORDE-UNNA road (inclusive) as their right boundary.

   (c) On "J plus 2" day the Lowland Division will sideslip to the east and take up the area shown in Map "A".

3. (a) The railways of primary importance in the British zone are

        (i) COLOGNE-OPLADEN-GRAFRATH-HAGEN-SCHWERTE-PADERBORN
             (HANNOVER 1/200000, Sheet 56).

        (ii) UNNA-SOEST-LIPPETADT (HANNOVER 1/200000, Sheet 56).

   (b) For the first stage of the advance troops of the VI British Corps will reach SOEST, those of the II Corps will reach UNNA, and those of the Belgian Army will reach HAMM.

4.   Table "A" attached gives a forecast of the moves and tasks of the various units of the Brigade Group, whose composition is shown in Table "B".

5./

5. (a) At 12 noon on "J minus 2" day the garrisons of the Posts found by the 8th K.O.S.B on the perimeter ll pass under the Command of the B.G.C. 1st Lowland Brigade, and those of the Posts found by the 11th Royal Scots under the Command of the B.G.C. 3rd Lowland Brigade. Details regarding the composition and situation of these Posts have been issued separately to 1st and 3rd Lowland Brigades.

   (b) On "J minus 1" day the garrisons of the Posts will be relieved by troops of the 2nd Highland Brigade (in the case of the 8th K.O.S.B.) and the 3rd Highland Brigade (in the case of the 11th Royal Scots) under arrangements to be made by 1st and 3rd Lowland Brigades respectively.

   Reliefs will be complete by 10.00 hours on "J minus 1" day, and troops relieved will rejoin their Battalions forthwith.

6. The Staff Captain, Civil Administration, will arrange to hand over by 12.00 hours on "J minus 2" day all details of the Civil Administration of WALD and GRAFRATH to 1st Lowland Brigade, and of OHLIGS and HAAN to 3rd Lowland Brigade, who will subsequently hand them over to the 2nd and 3rd Highland Brigades respectively.

7. During the preliminary concentration prior to "J" day the following troops will be moving into the present Brigade area, accommodation for whom will be allotted by the Staff Captain:-

On "J minus 3" Day.	1 Battn. 2nd Highland Bgde.	WALD.
"J minus 2" Day.	1 Battn. 3rd Highland Bgde.	OHLIGS.
"J minus 1" Day.	Composite Coy. from Corps Cyclist Battn. (less 1 platoon)	GRAFRATH *
" do. " Day.	9th Bn. M.G. Corps. (less 2 Coys.)	HAAN.
"	1 Coy. 9th Bn. M.G. Corps.	GRAFRATH *
" do. " Day.	1st Lowland Brigade Group.	GRAFRATH.
" do. " Day.	16th Bn. H.L.I. (Pioneers)	HAAN.
" do. " Day.	63rd Bgde. R.F.A. (less 1 Battery and 1 Section)	HAAN.

* These Units form part of 1st Lowland Brigade Group and accommodation for them will be sub-allotted by 1st Lowland Brigade.

8./

3.

8. (a) 1 Coy., 9th Battn., M.G. Corps and 1 platoon, Corps Cyclist Battalion, will be attached to the Brigade, reporting on "J minus 1" and "J minus 2" days respectively.

   (b) 1 section of machine guns, and 1 section of Cyclists will accompany the 6th K.O.S.B. and 11th Royal Scots on "J" day, and "J plus 1" day, and the 5th/6th Royal Scots and 11th Royal Scots on "J plus 2" day.

   On "J plus 2" day the section of machine guns and section of cyclists previously working with the 6th K.O.S.B. will rejoin their Coy. and platoon respectively.

9. B Battery, 51st Brigade, R.F.A. has been allotted to the Brigade. This will move as indicated in Table "A", remaining in Brigade Reserve to be used as circumstances may dictate.

10. 1 section, 90th Field Coy., R.E. will move with Brigade Headquarters and be kept in Brigade Reserve until its services are required for some definite purpose.

11. The 2nd Lowland T.M. Battery will be attached to the 11th Royal Scots for use, if necessary, in METTMANN on "J" and "J plus 1" days and in ELBERFELD on "J plus 2" day.

12. For "J" day and "J plus 1" day the 5th/6th Royal Scots will detail a platoon to move with and act as escort to Brigade Headquarters. On "J plus 2" day this platoon will be relieved by a similar party from 6th K.O.S.B.

13. (a) Administrative arrangements, and instructions in regard to civil administration are being issued separately.

    (b) Special instructions will also be issued with regard to the guarding of Railways, Power Stations, Telephone Exchanges and Water Supply.

14. (a) On "J" day, Brigade Headquarters will close at WALD and open at DORNAP. On "J plus 2" day it will close at DORNAP and open at ELBERFELD. Exact hours of opening and closing will be notified later.

    (b) Progress reports will be rendered frequently by all units of the Brigade Group.

15. ACKNOWLEDGE.

Captain,
Brigade Major,
2nd Lowland Brigade.

Copy No. 34

Issued at 1030 28/5/19.

Distribution :- See next page.

DISTRIBUTION.

Copy No. 1 to 11th Royal Scots.
      2 to 5/6th Royal Scots.
      3. " 6th K.O.S.B.
      4. " 2nd Lowland T.M. Battery.
      5. " 2nd Lowland Brigade School.
      6 & 7 to 51st Bde. R.F.A.
      8 & 9 to 9th Bn. M.G. Corps.
    10 & 11 to II Corps Cyclist Bn.
    12 to 27th Field Ambulance.
    13 to 106th Coy. R.A.S.C.
    14 to 90th Field Coy. R.E.
    15 to Staff Captain.
    16 to Staff Captain, Civil Administration.
    17 to Education Officer.
    18 to Brigade Signal Officer.
    19 to Intelligence Officer.
    20 to Brigade Transport Officer.
    21 to Lowland Divisional Train.
    22 to D.A.P.M.
    23 to Brigade Provost Officer.
    24 to Lowland Division "G".
    25 to   "   "   "Q".
    26 to 1st Lowland Brigade.
    27 to 3rd   "   "

    28 & 29 to WAR Diary.

Distribution of Map "A" and Map "B" :-

    5/6th Royal Scots.
    11th Royal Scots.
    6th K.O.S.B.
    2nd Lowland T.M. Battery.
    'B' Battery, 51st Bgde. R.F.A.
    'B' Coy. 9th Bn. M.G. Corps.
    Lowland Division.
    File.

TABLE "A".

Serial No.	Date.	Unit.	From.	To.	Route.	Task and Remarks.
1 (a)	J day.	8th KOSB.	WALD.	SCHOLLER-HAHNENFURTH area.	BISCHBACH.	(a) To occupy high ground N. and N.E. of (SQ.A.07) DUSSEL along the general line Pt.205(sq.A.27)- BERG(sq.A.17.) - SCHMUCK and cover the roads VELBERT - VOHWINKEL and WULFRATH - VOHWINKEL.
(b)		1 section "B"Coy.9th Bn. M.G.C.	HAAN.	Bn. Hdqrs. HAHNENFURTH.	POHLMUTZE.	
(c)		1 section Corps Cyclist Bn.	WALD.		TUNNEL at LINDEN. Road junct. in Sq.A.22.	(b) To keep touch with 11th Royal Scots at the high ground in square E.93, and with 51st H.L.I. (1st Lowland Brigade) at the bend in the road in sq.A.37. Area for which 5th K.O.S.B. will be responsible is shown on attached map "B".
2.(a)	J day.	Bde. H.Q.	WALD.	DORNAP.	SCHOLLER.	Instructions will be issued later as to the time the platoon of 5th/6th Royal Scots should report.
(b)		1 sect.90th Fd.Coy.RE.	WALD.		As for Serial 1.	
(c)		1 platoon 5/6 R.S.	OHLIGS.			
(d)		2 sectns. Corps Cyclist Bn.	WALD.			Will follow Serial 1.

Serial No.	Date.	Unit.	From	To.	Route.	Task and Remarks.
3 (a)	J day.	11th R.S.	HAAN.	METTMANN.	ELP.	(a) To make good the high ground N.W. of G... and subsequently, without delay, to occupy METTMANN.
(b)		1 Sect."B" Coy.9th Bn. M.G.C.	HAAN.	are.	GRUITEN.	(b) To occupy the high ground in Sq.E.96 to the WULFRATH-METTMANN Road and the general Pt.178(Sq.E.96)-Pt.155(Sq.E.65)-Pt.175(Sq... Hill.180(Sq.E. 84).
(c)		1 Sect. Corps Cyclist Bn.	WALD.	Battn. Bdqrs. METTMANN.		(c) To keep touch with I/4th R.S.F. 3rd Lowland Brigade about HUBBELRATH. Area for which 11th Royal Scots will be responsible is shown on attached map "P". On "J plus" day, or earlier, as soon as the Belgian forces have relieved them, the Royal Scots will withdraw from all position of the DUESSLDORF-METTMANN-WULFRATH road, a
(d)		2nd Lowland T.M. Bty.	WALD.			METTMANN itself, to accommodation S.E. of t... town suitably placed for the use, on "J plu... day, of the METTMANN-DORNAP-WEDEN-ELBERFEL... ROAD.
					HAAN.	To follow in rear of Serial 3 and march un... orders of 11th Royal Scots.
					ELP.	(a) To cover the approaches from VELBERT and WULFRATH and to dominate METTMANN.
4.	J day.	"B" Bty. 51st Bde. R.F.A.	K.2146 S.W. of HILDEN.	GRUITEN. Bty. H.Q. as arranged by O.C. But to be in touch by telephone with Bde.H.Q.	GRUITEN	(b) To be ready to support the infantry holding the line referred to in Serials 1 and 3.

* Touch will be obtained by means of a mounted officers patrol along the main METTMANN-D...
road, along which the 1/4th R.S.F. will s...
similar patrol.

APP. 2.

2nd LOWLAND BRIGADE.

MAY, 1919.

REINFORCEMENTS.

5/6th R.S.		11th R.S.		6th K.O.S.B.	
Off.	O.R.	Off.	O.R.	Off.	O.R.
5	57	2	22	6	99.

3.

Serial No.	Date.	Unit.	From.	To.	Route.	Task and Remarks.
5.	J day	1 Coy.(less 2 sections) 9th Bn. M.G.C.	HAAN.	GRUITEN Coy. Hdqrs. as arranged by O.C. but to be in touch by telephone with Bde. Hdqrs.	as for Serial 4.	To follow Serial 4 and march under orders of 11th Royal Scots.
6.	J day	5/6th R.S. (less 1 platoon)	OHLIGS.	GRUITEN area. Bn. Hdqrs. GRUITEN.	HAAN. ELP. GRUITEN.	To march in rear of Serial 5. Area for which 5/6th Royal Scots is responsible is shown on attached Map B.
7.	J day.	27th Fld. Ambulance. (less 1 Sectn.)	OHLIGS.	(Little) GRUITEN. E. 95.12.	HAAN. ELP.	To follow Serial 6 and march under orders of 5/6th Royal Scots.
8.	J day.	106th Coy. R.A.S.C.	WALD.	S.W. outskirts of VOHWINKEL.	As convenient exclusive of GRAFRATH- VOHWINKEL road.	To move as ordered by the Staff Captain, in rear of all previous serials.

Serial No.	Date.	Unit.	From.	To.	Route.	Task and Remarks.
9. (a)	J plus 2 day.	11th R.S.	METTMANN.	ELBERFELD area	DORNAP.	To occupy ELBERFELD and high ground N. of it in vicinity of Pts. 291 and 303 - taking over from Pts. 291 and 303 - taking over from 51st H.L.I. and 15th H.L.I. (1st Lowland Brigade)
(b)		1 Sectn. 'B' Coy. 9th Bn. M.G.C.	area	Bn. H.Q. ELBERFELD.	WIEDEN.	
(c)		1 Sectn. Corps Cyclist Bn.				
(d)		2nd Lowland T.M. Bty.				
10.	J plus 2 day.	B Bty. 51st Bde. R.F.A.	GRUITEN.	Northern Outskirts of ELBERFELD.	POTHERBRUCK (Sq.E.82) SCHOLLERSHEIDE (Sq.A.04) thence as for Serial 9.	To follow immediately in rear of serial 9 from SCHOLLERS HEIDE and march under orders of 11th Royal Scots.
11. (a)	J plus 2 day.	Bgde. Hdqrs.	DORNAP.	ELBERFELD.	WIEDEN.	To take over from 1st Lowland Brigade Brigade Hdqrs. in ELBERFELD.
(b)		1 Sectn. 90th Fld. Coy. R.E.				To follow Serial 10.
(c)		1 platoon, 6th K.O.S.B.				
(d)		2 Sectns. Corps Cyclist Bn.				

Serial No.	Date.	Unit.	From	To.	Route.	Task and Remarks.
12. (a)	J plus 2 day	5/6th R.S.	GRUITEN	CRONENBERG area	VOHWINKEL - SONNBORN	To occupy CRONENBERG taking over from 5th K.O.S.B.(1st Lowland Bde.)
(b)		1 Sectn. 'B' Coy.9th Bn. M.G.Corps				
(c)		1 Sectn. Corps Cyclist Bn.				
13.	J plus 2 day	5th K.O.S.B. (less 1 platoon)	SCHOLLER HAHNENFURTH	VOHWINKEL.	DORNAP WIEDEN	To concentrate and be in Bgde. reserve.
14.	J plus 2 day	'B' Coy. 9th Bn M.G.C. (less 3 Sectns)	GRUITEN.	SONNBORN.	VOHWINKEL. SONNBORN.	To follow immediately in rear of Serial 12 and march under orders of 5/6th Royal Scots.
15.	J plus 2 day	27th Fld. Ambulence. (less 1 Sectn)	(Little) GRUITEN. E. 9512.	VOHWINKEL.	GRUITEN.	To follow immediately in rear of Serial 14 and march under orders of 5/6th Royal Scots.
16.	J plus 2 day	106th Coy. R.A.S.C.				To move to vicinity of railhead under orders to be issued by Staff Captain.

NOTES. (i) Every column is responsible for its own protection both on the march and when halted.
(ii) Should the normal telephone service fail, it is possible that communication may be established on "J" and "J plus 1" days along the railway between METTMANN and DORNAP.

TABLE "B" to accompany 2nd LOWLAND BRIGADE ORDER No. 2.
dated 26th May, 1919.

═══

2nd LOWLAND BRIGADE.

    2nd Lowland Brigade H.Q.
    5/6th Royal Scots.
    11th Royal Scots.
    6th K.O.S.B.
    2nd Lowland T.M. Battery.
    27th Field Ambulance.(Less 1 Section).
    1 Section, 90th Field Coy. R.E.
    106th Coy. Div. Train.
    'B' Battery, 51st Bgde. R.F.A.
    'B' Coy. 9th Bn. M.G.C.
    1 Platoon Cyclists.

All Recipients of 2nd Lowland Brigade Order No. 2.

    Herewith Table 'B' to accompany 2nd Lowland Brigade Order No. 2 dated yesterday.

                              C.A.Ryan
                                Captain,
                            Brigade Major,
27th May, 1919.   2nd Lowland Brigade.

Secret

Amendment No. 1 to 2nd Lowland Brigade Order No. 2.
==

1. The plan of advance of the Belgians has been modified by the arrival of the 33rd French Corps. The new arrangements are as follows :-

    On "J" day a Belgian Division moves to area W. of HAMM and a French Division to the area DORTMUND - UNNA by ~~Battalions~~.

    French and Belgian cavalry reach the line WITTEN - BOCHUM.

    The 46th French Division will be immediately N. of the Lowland Division in the area RATINGEN - WULFRATH - VELBERT - HATTINGEN.

2. In consequence of this, the last 4 lines of para. 2(b) of the above order and Maps A & B will be amended to show the DUSSELDORF-METTMANN - WULFRATH road inclusive to 2nd Brigade - METTMANN inclusive and WULFRATH exclusive.

    The last 8 lines of "Remarks" Column for Serial 3 are also cancelled.

3. In the route column for Serial 12, after SONNBORN add ELBERFELD.

4. Map B will be amended so as to make HOCHDAHL and MILLRATH inclusive to the 5/6th Royal Scots., and VOHWINKEL exclusive to 6th K.O.S.B. and inclusive to the 1st Lowland Brigade.

5. In "Remarks" column Serial 12 delete " taking over from 5th K.O.S.B. (1st Lowland Brigade)".

    Note.   The 5th K.O.S.B. will be in VOHWINKEL and SONNBORN on "J plus 1" day.

                                                    Captain,
                                                 Brigade Major,
                                               2nd Lowland Brigade.

SECRET.

ADDENDUM No. 2 to 2nd LOWLAND BRIGADE ORDER No.2.
==

1. NOTIFICATION OF "J" DAY.

   The following code will be used to notify "J" day to units of the 2nd Lowland Brigade Group :-

   If "J" day is, for example, June 3rd a code message will be sent ONOTO 3. If it is June 5th, then the message will be ONOTO 5 and so on.

   The code word for the month of July will be SWAN, and for August WATERMAN.

2. MAPS.

   Orders from Brigade Headquarters will refer to the METTMANN and ELBERFELD sheets 1/25,000 or to the 1/200,000 series.

3. ROYAL AIR FORCE.

   (a) Machines flying over the Divisional Front will belong to the 7th Squadron, R.A.F., whose Headquarters will remain at MULHEIM.

   (b) One contact patrol machine and one counter attack patrol machine will operate on the front from "J" day onwards.

   (c) Popham Panels will always be displayed at Report Centres of Brigade H.Q. and Battalion H.Q., and the Brigade Signal Officer will ensure that Battalions are in possession of the necessary panels and have men trained in their use.

4. INTELLIGENCE PERSONNEL.

   A certain number of intelligence personnel will accompany leading Battalions and they will be responsible for seizing "suspects" in the area to be occupied. Guards must be provided by Battalions concerned if application for them is made.

5. COMMUNICATIONS.

   (a) Copies of 4 letter code calls for use at wireless stations will be issued on "J minus 1" day to all concerned.

   (b) A Brigade Report Centre will be established at LOOP POST, (A.12.09) before the commencement of operations on "J" day, and will remain there until Brigade Headquarters is opened, on completion of the move, at DORNAP.

   Messages carried by runners should be sent to Brigade Headquarters in its place in the column on the march, but telephone messages and wires can be sent to the Report Centre at LOOP POST.

6. CONTROL OVER RAILWAYS.

(a) One of the principal objectives of the first stage of the advance is to secure complete control over the German railway systems that are considered essential for a further advance.

The railways of primary importance in the British zone are those given in para. 3(a) of 2nd Lowland Brigade Order No. 2 of 26/5/19.

(b) The essential measures to be taken in the first instance by advancing troops to achieve this object are :-

To occupy stations and important junctions; to prevent any destruction of material or escape of personnel; to put up proclamations of which copies will be provided; to occupy the head railway offices of towns and stations and to compel German personnel to remain at their posts, more especially head manager, sub-managers, and station masters, who should be held responsible for the good behaviour of the subordinate employees; and to stop all movement of trains until the control of the general management has been taken over by the Inter-Allied Railway Commission.

(c) All concerned will be notified when the Inter-Allied Railway Commission has taken over the management of the railways and, after this, no railway trains, telephones, telegraphs, buildings, or officials are to be interfered with, although the latter may, for a short time, be without passes.

(d) The representative of the Inter-Allied Railway Commission for the II Corps will be located at ELBERFELD and, together with his staff will be moving with the advanced troops, so as to establish his Headquarters as early as possible.

(e) With reference to para. (b) above, Battalions of this Brigade will be responsible for dealing on "J" day with stations as under :-

5/6th Royal Scots.	(HOCHDAHL. (GRUITEN.
11th Royal Scots.	METTMANN.
6th K.O.S.B.	(DORNAP. (HAHNENFURTH.

7. INTELLIGENCE.

Circulars are attached (to recipients of Map "B") showing important works, etc., in the various towns in the area to be occupied together with information concerning billeting possibilities.

Plans of towns in this area will be forwarded in due course when received.

A note on the water supply in area E. and N.E. of the COLOGNE Bridgehead is forwarded herewith to Battalions only.

Captain,
Brigade Major,
2nd Lowland Brigade.

Distribution :- All Recipients of 2nd Lowland Brigade Order No. 2 of 26/5/19.

2 MBde

H.Q. 2nd Low. BDE

WAR DIARY

or

INTELLIGENCE SUMMARY.

(Erase heading not required.)

Army Form C. 2118.

1st June 1919

Place	Date	Hour	Summary of Events and Information	Remarks and references to Appendices
VILLA KORTENBACH	2.6.19		The Commander in Chief, British Army of the Rhine inspected 5/6 Royal Scots on their Parade ground at Schutzenberg at 11.30 a.m.	
89 WEYER OHLIGS	12.6.19		Brigade Commander inspected 6th K.O.S.B. on their Battalion Parade Ground at 2720.2272 their Turnfest, and wrestler killed.	
RHINELAND GERMANY	14.6.19		A meeting of sports officers was held at Bde H.Q. at 14.30 hours amendments No. 2 to 2nd Lowland Bde order No. 2 dated 26.5.19 issued – 1 Capt. E.B. Isaacson M.C. F.S.O. 3 & 4th Bn © arrives awaiting orders of this Major. 2nd Lowland Bde over Captain E.R. Ryan D.S.O. M.C.	APP 1
	16.6.19 17.6.19		© nd Command visited Battn H.Q rs at 10.00 hours to see the amendments No 3 & 4 and addendum No 4 3 & 2 nd Lowland Bde order No. 2 dated 26.5.19 issued 2nd Lowland Brigade order No. 3 issued giving details of advance and notes to be taken when new frontier reached.	APP 2
	23.6.19		Wire received Stopping any further advance. 2nd Lowland Brigade Order No. 4 issued to all concerned, giving final instructions as to forward movement	APP 3
	24.6.19		Telegram received from Divison stating that the Germans had decided to sign the Peace Treaty	APP 4
	25.6.19		Instructions issued for return of split Nation attached to 2nd Lowland Bde to their section at present Brigade Order No. 5 issued to all concerned regarding movement of troops of Highland Division back to their original location in Zone of Rhine Army and	APP 5

Army Form C. 2118.

WAR DIARY for June 1919
INTELLIGENCE SUMMARY

(Erase heading not required.)

Place	Date	Hour	Summary of Events and Information	Remarks and references to Appendices
VILLA KORTENBACH	27.6.19		Amendment to Brigade Order No. 5 issued	APP. 6
89 W EYER OHLIGS	28.6.19		Wire received from D. notifying that Peace had been signed and that troops of Highland D. would return to original locations commencing 30th June.	
RHINELAND GERMANY	30.6.19		March of Highland D. was carried out in accordance with instructions issued on 28th June.	APP. 7
			Reinforcements	

Signed,
Brigade Major
2nd Lowland Brigade

War D copy

SECRET.
Copy No. 31

27th June, 1919.

AMENDMENT TO 2ND LOWLAND BRIGADE ORDER NO.5.

1. Para. 2. for " B day is ...." read " A day is ...."

2. Para.3. Cancel first sub-para. and substitute:-

    " The 11th Royal Scots will relieve the 4th Seaforth Highlanders in the left sub-sector on "A" day. Relief to be complete by 18.00 hours. The 6th K.O.S.B. will relieve the 5th Gordon Highlanders in the right sub-sector on "C" day. Relief to be complete by 09.00 hours."

    Para. 3, sub-para. 3 For " On "B" day the bridge guards" read " On "A" day the bridge guards".

3. Para . 5. The Civil Administration of the CHLIGS-HAAN Area will be taken over by 2nd Lowland Brigade from 3rd Highland Brigade on "A" day. The handing over to be completed by 18.00 hours.

4. ACKNOWLEDGE. (Units of Bde Group + 3rd Highland Bde only)

                                    Captain,
                              Brigade Major,
                            2nd Lowland Brigade.

Copy to all Recipients of
2nd Lowland Brigade Order No.5.

War Diary

SECRET.

2ND LOWLAND BRIGADE ORDER NO. 5.

Copy No. 31
25th June, 1919.

1. In the event of orders being issued for the return of troops to their original locations, the 2nd Lowland Brigade will take over its original sector in the Perimeter from troops of the 2nd and 3rd Highland Brigades on "C" and "B" days respectively.

2. Units will be prepared to carry out these moves on receipt of a wire from Brigade H.Q. as follows, " B day is .... ".

3. The 6th K.O.S.B. will relieve the 5th Gordon Highlanders in the right sub-sector and the 11th Royal Scots the 4th Seaforth Highlanders in the left sub-sector. Reliefs to be completed by 09.00 hours on "C" and "B" days respectively.

All details of relief will be arranged direct between Commanding Officers concerned.

On "B" day the bridge guard at OHLIGS will be taken over by 5/6th Royal Scots from 1/4th Seaforth Highlanders, strength of guard, 2 sections ; and the Bridge guards at HAAN by the 11th Royal Scots, strength of guard, 1 platoon. Reliefs to be completed by 09.00 hours.

4. All Defence Plans, Maps, Ammunition, Requisitioned stores, etc. will be handed over on relief, and receipts given. Copies of these receipts will be forwarded to Bde. H.Q.

5. The Civil Administration of the WALD-GRAFRATH and the OHLIGS-HAAN Areas will be taken over by 2nd Lowland Bde. from the 2nd and 3rd Highland Brigades, respectively. Handing over to be completed by 12.00 hours on "B" day.

These two areas will then be amalgamated into No. 2 Sub-Area as heretofore.

6. The Brigade Provost Officer will arrange to take over the Tramway Control at KLUSE POST and LOOP POST by 09.00 hours on "B" day. The provost personnel which has been returned to Battalions will be ordered to rejoin the Provost Office Staff under orders to be issued later.

7. Progress and completion of moves and relief will be wired to Brigade H.Q.

8. ACKNOWLEDGE.

Captain
Brigade Major,
Distribution :-(see overleaf). 2nd Lowland Brigade.

DISTRIBUTION.

Copy No.
1 to 5/6th Royal Scots.
2 to 11th Royal Scots.
3 to 6th K.O.S.B.
4 to 2nd Lowland T.M.B.
5 to 2nd Lowland Bde. School.
6 & 7 to 51st Bde. R.F.A.
8 & 9 to Lowland Bn. M.G.C.
10 to 27th Field Ambulance.
11 to 105th Coy. R.A.S.C.
12 to 90th Field Coy. R.E.
13 to G.O.C.
14 to Brigade Major.
15 to Staff Captain.
16 to Staff Captain, C.A.
17 to Education Officer.
18 to Brigade Signal Officer.
19 to Intelligence Officer.
20 to Bde. Transport Officer.
21 to Lowland Div. Train.
22 to D.A.P.M., Lowland Division.
23 to Bde. Provost Officer.
24 to Lowland Division "G".
25 to   do.   do.   "Q".
26 to 1st Lowland Brigade.
27 to 3rd Lowland Brigade.
28 to 16th H.L.I.
29 to 2nd Highland Brigade.
30 to 3rd Highland Brigade.
31 & 32 to War Diary.
33 to File.

War Diary

2nd LOWLAND BRIGADE ORDER No. 4.

SECRET.
Copy No......

1. All preparations will be made to commence the moves laid down for J day at 03.15 hours, 24th June, which hour will be zero hour.

2. The head of each column of the Brigade Group will pass its starting point as follows :-

    No. 1 Column   Zero.
    No. 2.   "   Zero plus 20 mins.
    No. 3.   "   Zero plus 30 mins.
    No. 4.   Zero minus 30 mins.

3. No movement will take place until receipt of the following Urgent Operations Priority message : COMMENCE MARCH ~~~~ 24th and ACKNOWLEDGE.
    Possibly this message may not be sent out from Brigade H.Q. before 23.00 hours on 23rd.

    From noon onwards to-day an officer must be in the Office of each Unit.

4. As soon as troops of the Lowland Division have passed the Perimeter Posts, Units of the Highland Division will be withdrawn and concentrated.

5. 5/6th Royal Scots will attach one Platoon complete with Lewis guns to Lowland Division M.T. Coy at SCHOOL MERSCHEID, OHLIGS.
    This Platoon will report to Division M.T. Column by 19.00 hours on 23rd and be prepared to commence escort duty of the M.T. Column on "J" Day.

6. Contact aeroplanes of the 7th Squadron, R.A.F. will fly a yellow and red streamer from their tails and will also carry black flaps attached to the rear edge of the lower plane, one on each side of the body.

7. Brigade Report Centre will open at KLUSE POST at 03.00 hours.

8. Progress Reports will be rendered frequently to Bde. H.Q.

9. ACKNOWLEDGE.

Issued through Signals
    at 13.45 hours.

Distributed to all Recipients
of 2nd Lowland Brigade Order No.2.

Captain,
Brigade Major,
2nd Lowland Brigade.

War Diary

SECRET.
Copy No. ......
19/6/19.

2ND LOWLAND BRIGADE ORDER NO. 3.

Ref. 1/200,000, COLN (Sheet 59).
    do.   MUNSTER (Sheet 55).
SOLINGEN)
  and   ) 1/25,000.
ELBERFELD)

1. The 2nd Lowland Brigade Group will advance on "J" day in 4 columns in accordance with Table "C" attached.

2. The 1st Lowland Brigade is advancing on "J" day and occupying ELBERFELD and the high ground on the general line A. 9595, A.8690 - A.7880 - A.6080 - A. 5680 - A.4575 and A. 3775.

    This advance will be carried out covered by an advance guard composed of the following Units :-
    3 platoons, 8th Cyclist Bn.
    "A" Battery, 50th Bde. R.F.A.
    15th Bn. H.L.I.

    The 2nd Lowland Brigade will be in support of 1st Lowland Brigade and will be prepared to render any assistance that may be called for.

3. On arrival at their stations each Battalion will detail 1 Company as an Inlying Picquet. Other Units will detail a picquet of 25% of their strength.

    These Picquets must be ready to turn out immediately on the ALARM being given.

4. An Alarm Post will be selected by each Unit and its locality made known to all ranks.

5. Units on arrival will notify the position of their H.Q. and ALARM Post to Brigade H.Q.

6. Orders re the synchronization of watches will be notified later.

7. A C K N O W L E D G E.

Captain,
Brigade Major,
2nd Lowland Brigade.

DISTRIBUTION.(See overleaf).

DISTRIBUTION.

Copy No. 1 to 11th Royal Scots.
       2 to 5/6th Royal Scots.
       3 to 6th K.O.S.B.
       4 to 2nd Lowland T.M.B.
       5 to 2nd Lowland Brigade School.
       6 & 7 to 51st Brigade R.F.A.
       8 & 9 to 9th Bn. M.G.C.
     10 & 11 to II Corps Cyclist Bn.
     12 to 27th Field Ambulance.
     13 to 106th Coy. R.A.S.C.
     14 to 90th Field Coy. R.E.
     15 to Staff Captain.
     16 to Staff Captain, Civil Administration.
     17 to Education Officer.
     18 to Brigade Signal Officer.
     19 to Intelligence Officer.
     20 to Brigade Transport Officer.
     21 to Lowland Divisional Train.
     22 to D.A.P.M.
     23 to Brigade Provost Officer.
     24 to Lowland Division "G".
     25 to   "   "   "Q".
     26 to 1st Lowland Brigade.
     27 to 3rd Lowland Brigade.
     28 & 29 to War Diary.
     30 to 16th H.L.I.

TABLE "C".

Column.	Serial No. in Table "A" of Bde. Order No. 2.	Under Orders of.	Route.	Starting Point.	Time.	Remarks.
1.	1, 2, and 3.	O.C., 11th Royal Scots.	HAAN-POLNMUTZE	Road Junction ROTZCHEN K. 9896.	Zero.	Troops of this column halting in VORWINKEL must be clear of the GRAFRATH-WULFRATH Road.
2.	4.	O.C., 6th H.O.S.B.	CENTRAL-GRAFRATH-VORWINKEL.	Bridge where the SOLINGEN-GRAFRATH Railway Crosses or the WALD-KETZBERG Road. F.24 78	Zero plus 20.	
3.	5 and 6.	Bde. H.Q.	do.	do.	Zero plus 30.	
4.	7 and 8.	O.C., 5/8th Royal Scots.	HAAN-POLNMUTZE	Road Junction TROTZ-HILDEN K. 7556.	Zero minus 30	

Serial No. 9 will march in rear of the Brigade Group under orders to be issued by the Staff Captain. Zero hour will be notified later.

SECRET.

To All Recipients of 2nd Lowland
              Brigade Order No. 2 dated 26/5/19.

AMENDMENT NO. 4.

Cancel sub-para. (e) of para.6, Addendum No. 2 to 2nd Lowland Brigade Order No. 2.

[signature]
Captain,
Brigade Major,
2nd Lowland Brigade.

War Diary

SECRET.

ADDENDUM NO. 4 TO 2ND LOWLAND BRIGADE ORDER NO. 2 DATED 26/5/19.
===

1. On and after "J" day Situation Reports will be rendered to Brigade H.Q. as under :-

   (a) **Morning Situation Report.**

   Daily (by wire) so as to reach Brigade H.Q. by 05.00 hours.

   (b) **Evening Situation Report.** (including prisoners of war and material captured).

   Daily (by wire) so as to reach Brigade H.Q. by 14.00 hours.

2. **INTELLIGENCE SUMMARIES AND REPORTS.**

   (a) Priority wire giving unit of any prisoners captured as soon after capture as possible.

   (b) Daily Intelligence Summaries are required for the period from 20.00 to 20.00 hours. These will be forwarded

(1) For period 20.00 hours to 16.00 hours.	By runner to reach Brigade H.Q. by 16.30 hours.
(2) For period 16.00 hours to 20.00 hours.	By wire or telephone to reach Brigade H.Q. by 21.00 hours.

3. **PROCLAMATIONS.**

   The following proclamations have been issued to Units of the Brigade Group :-
   (a) "Order to the Civil Population".
   (b) "Order to facilitate the work of the Armies and in the interest of the Civil Population.".

   No use is to be made of these proclamations before "J" day, but as soon as the advance commences they will be freely distributed and posted up as widely as possible.

4./ **MARCH DISCIPLINE.**

   All ranks are to pay the strictest attention to march discipline. The usual 10 minute halts before each clock hour will be observed.

   A motor ambulance will follow the troops marching by the GRAFRATH Road and also those proceeding by HAAN. No troops will be allowed to enter these ambulances unless they are in possession of a certificate stating they are unable to march, signed by the Regimental Medical Officer.

5./

5. BOUNDARIES.

On "J" day and "J plus 1" day the boundary with the 1st Lowland Infantry Brigade will be the road from the Railway Crossing at A. 62.57 - through WARRESBECK - Road junction at A. 61.43, all inclusive to 1st Brigade.

6. LIAISON.

Orders have been issued by General MICHEL to the 33rd French Corps that throughout the march on "J" day, liaison must be made by cyclists with the British Army on the WULFRATH-GRAFRATH Road.

O.C., 6th K.O.S.B. will, after his column has passed VOHWINKEL, gain touch with the French on this Road by means of cyclists attached to his column.

7. Add new sub-para(e) to para.6 of Addendum No. 2 of 2nd Lowland Brigade Order No. 2.

(e) With reference to para.(b) above, Battalions of this Brigade will be responsible for dealing on "J" day with stations as under :-

5/6th Royal Scots.	VOHWINKEL.
11th Royal Scots.	SONNBORN.

8. Battalions will also be responsible for safeguarding the following vulnerable points :-

5/6th Royal Scots.	The Bridges at A. 3433.
	A. 3629.
	A. 4234.
	A. 3226.
	The tunnel at TESCHE. A. 3739
11th Royal Scots	The Bridges at A. 5538.
	A. 5638.
	A. 5839.
	The Gas Works.
6th K.O.S.B.	The Bridges at A. 4645.
	A. 5754.

Officers Commanding will, on the arrival of their Battalion cause a reconnaissance of the railways to be made so as to ensure that all vulnerable points are adequately protected.

9. Serial No. 1(c) of Table A attached to Brigade Order No.2 Column "FROM" for "WALD" read "HAAN".

10./

- 3 -

10. GUARDING OF TELEPHONES

The Brigade Signal Officer will detail personnel to take over telephone offices as follows :-

1 N.C.O.& 5 men.   to VOHWINKEL.
1 N.C.O.& 5 men   to SONNBORN.

The 1 N.C.O. and 5 men for SONNBORN will be detailed by 11th Royal Scots. Instructions will be sent by wire as to the time they are to report at Brigade Signal Office.

These men will march with the 1st Lowland Brigade Group.

On arrival at the above mentioned places they will take over and secure the offices. German personnel, especially the postmasters, must be forced to remain at their offices. All civilian signal traffic must be stopped by means other than the destruction of lines and instruments. No German personnel is to be allowed to touch any signal apparatus except in the presence of a representative of the Signal Service.

11.   ACKNOWLEDGE.

Captain,
Brigade Major,
2nd Lowland Brigade.

Copies to all Recipients of 2nd Lowland Brigade
            Order No.2 dated 26/5/19.

ADDENDUM NO.3 TO 2ND LOWLAND BRIGADE ORDER NO.2 DATED 26/5/19.

1. Add Sub-Para. (d) to para.3 "ROYAL AIR FORCE" of Addendum No. 2 as follows :-

   (d) During the advance Red Very Lights (1") will be used by the Infantry as a signal to indicate that their advance is being resisted by the enemy.

2. Add new para.8 to Addendum No. 2 as under :-

   (8) DIVISIONAL COLLECTING STATION.

   Divisional Collecting Station for prisoners and documents will be at BRAFRATH from "J minus 2" day inclusive.

3. ACKNOWLEDGE.

Brigade Major,
2nd Lowland Brigade.

Copies to all Recipients of 2nd Lowland
Brigade Order No. 2 Dated 26/5/19.

SECRET.

AMENDMENT NO.3 TO 2ND LOWLAND BRIGADE ORDER NO.2 DATED 26/5/19.

Para.5 (b) first and last lines for "LOOP POST(A. 12.09)" read "KLUSE POST(A.36.14)".

For "DORNAP" read "VOHWINKEL."

Captain,
Brigade Major,
2nd Lowland Brigade.

Copies to all Recipients of 2nd Lowland
    Brigade Order No.2.

File

SECRET.

All Recipients of 2nd Lowland
  Brigade Order No. 2 dated 26/5/19.
----

1.   Herewith amendment No. 2 to 2nd Lowland Brigade Order No.2 dated 26/5/19, and a new Table A to be substituted for that issued with above mentioned order.

2.   The net effect of these changes is that, as the Franco-Belgian forces are now taking over the whole of DUSSELDORF, the 3rd Lowland Brigade will occupy the area previously allotted to this Brigade.

    As a result, the 2nd Brigade for "J" and "J plus 1" days is concentrated in the area VOHWINKEL-SONNBORN, to which area it will move as soon as possible in rear of the 1st Lowland Brigade, moving on "J plus 2" day to the area CRONENBERG-ELBERFELD-DONBERG-NEVIGES.

[signature]
Captain,
Brigade Major,
2nd Lowland Brigade.

AMENDMENT NO. 2 TO 2ND LOWLAND BRIGADE ORDER NO.2   SECRET.
      DATED 26TH MAY, 1919.
_____

1.   In para.2 (a) line 2 for " METTMANN - DUSSELDORF " read
"METTMANN(exclusive) - DUSSELDORF(exclusive)".

2.   In para.2 (b) delete the line therein given as the right
boundary of the Franco-Belgian forces and substitute:-

   " DUSSELDORF GEMEINDE boundary to stream E. of GLASHUTTE -
     thence along stream to METTMANN(inclusive to Franco-Belgian
     forces) - NEVIGES(inclusive to British forces) - LANGENBERG
     (inclusive to Franco-Belgian forces) - then along LANGENBERG-
     HATTINGEN- WITTEN-HORDE-UNNA Road(inclusive to Franco-Belgian
     forces) ".

3.   Para.2 (c) is cancelled.

4.   Delete para.8 (b) and substitute:-

   " 1 section Machine gunners and 1 section of cyclists will
     accompany 6th K.O.S.B. and 11th Royal Scots on "J" day and
     "J plus 1" day.
     Allotment for "J plus 2" day will be made later. "

5.   Delete para. 11. The 2nd Lowland T.M. Battery will move
as a complete unit with Brigade H.Q.

6.   Para.12 . Delete " On "J plus 2" day this platoon will be
relieved by a similar party from 6th K.O.S.B."

7.   In para.14 (a) for " DONNAP" read "VOHWINKEL".

8.   Herewith fresh Table B to be substituted for that issued
with 2nd Lowland Brigade Order No.2 dated 26/5/19.

9.   Map B issued with 2nd Lowland Brigade Order No.2 dated
26/5/19 is cancelled and a trace to superimpose on Map A is
attached showing the boundary referred to in para.2 above.
        The Brigade areas in Map A are now obsolete.

                                            Captain,
                                         Brigade Major,
                                        2nd Lowland Brigade.

12th June, 1919.

Copy to all Recipients of 2nd Lowland
   Brigade Order No. 2 dated 26/5/19.

TABLE "A".

Serial. No.	Date.	Unit.	From.	To.	Route.	Task and Remarks.
1.(a)	J Day	11th R.S.	HAAN			
(b)		1 sect. "B" Coy. 9th Bn. M.G.C.	HAAN	SONNBORN.	via VOHWINKEL.	
(c)		1 Sect. Corps Cyclist Bn.	WALD			
2.	J Day	1 Coy. (less 2 Sects.)9th Bn. M.G.C.	HAAN.	VOHWINKEL	as for Serial 1.	To follow Serial 1 and march under orders of 11th Royal Scots.
3.	J Day	"B" Bty. 51st Bde. R.F.A.	K.21.46 S.W. of HILDEN.	VOHWINKEL	via HAAN	To follow in rear of Serial 2 and march under orders of 11th Royal Scots.
4.(a)	J Day	6th K.O.S.B.	WALD.			
(b)		2 Sect. "B" Coy. 9th Bn. M.G.C.	HAAN	WIEDEN - SACKSENHAUS (Sq.A.35 Sq.A.55).	GRAFRATH VOHWINKEL.	
(c)		1 Sect.Corps Cyclist.Bn.	WALD.			
5.(a)	J Day	Bde. H.Q.	WALD.	VOHWINKEL	As for Serial 4.	Instructions will be issued later as to the time the platoon of 5/6th Royal Scots should report. Will follow Serial 4.
(b)		1 sect. 90th Fd.Coy.R.E.	WALD.			
(c)		1 platoon 5/6th R.S.	OHLIGS.			
(d)		2 Sects. Corps Cyclist Bn.	WALD.			

- 2 -

Serial No.	Date.	Unit.	From.	To.	Route.	Task and Remarks.
6.	J Day.	2nd Lowld. T.M.B.	WALD	VOHWINKEL.	as for Serial 4.	Will follow Serial 5.
7.	J Day.	5/6th R.S. (less 1 platoon)	OHLIGS.	VOHWINKEL	via HAAN	
8.	J Day.	27th Fd. Ambulance (less 1 Section)	OHLIGS.	VOHWINKEL.	via HAAN	To follow Serial 7, and march under orders of 5/8th Royal Scots.
9.	J Day.	106th Coy. R.A.S.C.	WALD.	S.W.Outskirts ofVOHWINKEL.	via GRAFRATH.	To move as ordered by the Staff Capt. in rear of all previous Serials.
10.(a)	J plus 2 Day	A Battn.		CRONENBERG		
(b)		1 Sect. 'B' Coy. 9thBN.M.G.C.				
(c)		1 Sect.Corps Cyclist Bn.				
11.(a)	J plus 2 day	B Battn.		SONBERG.		
(b)		1 Sect.'B' Coy.9th Bn. M.G.C.				
(c)		1 Sect. Corps Cyclist Bn.				
12.	J plus 2 day.	C Battn.		ELBERFELD.		
13.(a)						

- 3 -

Serial No.	Date.	Unit.	From.	To.	Route.	Task and Remarks.
13.(a)	J plus 2 day.	Bde. H.Q.	VOHWINKEL.	ELBERFELD	via SONNBORN	To take over from 1st Lowland Brigade. Brigade H.Q. in ELBERFELD.
(b)		1 Sect. 90th Fd. Coy. RE.				
(c)		1 platoon Escort				
(d)		2 Sections Corps Cyclist Bn.				
14.	J plus 2 day.	2nd Lowland T.M.Bty.	VOHWINKEL	ELBERFELD	via SONNBORN.	To follow Serial 13.
15.	J plus 2 day	'B' Coy. 9th Bn. M.G.C. (less 2 Sects.)	VOHWINKEL	ELBERFELD	via SONNBORN.	To follow immediately in rear of Serial 14.
16.	J plus 2 day	'B' Bty. 51st Bde. R.F.A.	VOHWINKEL	ELBERFELD		To follow Serial 15.
17.	J plus 2 day	27th Fd. Ambulance (less 1 Sect)	VOHWINKEL	SONNBORN		To follow immediately in rear of Serial 15.
18.	J plus 2 day	105th Coy. R.A.S.C.				To move to vicinity of Railhead under orders to be issued by Staff Capt.

NOTES:/

- 4 -

NOTES.

(i) Every column is responsible for its own protection both on the march and when halted.

(ii) On "J" Day and "J plus 1" day the 2nd Lowland Brigade will be concentrated ready to support the 1st Lowland Brigade, if necessary, in ELBERFELD, BARMEN or CRONENBERG.

(iii) Final Areas of Brigades will be as follows :-

3rd Lowland Brigade. The Area West of the GRAFRATH-VOHWINKEL-WULFRATH Road exclusive, including the Gemeindes of SCHOLLER, GRUITEN, MILLRATH and ERKRATH.

2nd Lowland Brigade. From the GRAFRATH-VOHWINKEL-WULFRATH Road inclusive, eastward to include the Gemeindes of CRONENBERG, ELBERFELD, DONBERG, and NEVIGES.

1st Lowland Brigade. BARMEN and the remainder of the Lowland Divisional area to the east, including the Gemeindes of BARMEN, SCHWELM, GEBBESBERG, and Ndr. and Obr. SRROCKHOVEL.

B.M.18.
4th August, 1919.

Lowland Division.

Herewith War Diaries of Brigade H.Q. and three battalions of this Brigade for July, 1919.

Please acknowledge.

S.C. Collier Capt.,
Staff. Capt.
2nd Lowland Brigade.
for Brigadier-General,
Commanding 2nd Lowland Brigade.

REINFORCEMENTS.

5/6th R.SCOTS.		11th R.SCOTS.		6th. K.O.S.B.	
Off.	O.R.	Off.	O.R.	Off.	O.R.
1	9	3	4	1	24

Army Form C. 2118.

WAR DIARY for July 1919
or
INTELLIGENCE/SUMMARY.
(Erase heading not required.)

Instructions regarding War Diaries and Intelligence Summaries are contained in F. S. Regs., Part II. and the Staff Manual respectively. Title pages will be prepared in manuscript.

Place	Date	Hour	Summary of Events and Information	Remarks and references to Appendices
Gill	July 3		Brigadier General R. Kenyon Forces, C.M.G., D.S.O. resumes command of Brigade	
Rhineland			Vice Brigadier Samuel C.B. Loch, C.M.G., D.S.O. proceeding to England to take over command of 1st Battalion The Royal Scots.	
Germany				
Sheet 3 R.M.M.	5		Warned warning units that Brigade moves on Tuesday 8th inst.	
1:25000	6		Brigade School closes and Staff return to their units.	
N. 6704			Warned moved from Donnar Kaffernay move 8th 24 hours	
	7		2nd Rowland Brigade Order N° 6 issued giving details of move to area of 2nd Light Brigade	App. I
	8		Attention N° 1. to 2nd Rowland Brigade Order N° 6 issued	App. II
	12		A conference of Battalion Commanders at B.H.Q at 12.00 hrs re training in new area	
	14		Divisional Commander inspected all units of the Brigade.	
			Captain S.E. Collins M.C. assumes duties of Staff Captain vice Capt R Duckie M.C. to Kenkart Division as D.A.A.S.	
	19		Heard of Corps Commander to 2.N.Q Battalion C Oak met Hamel 12.00 hrs	
	29		The Commander in Chief British Army of the Rhine inspects the C.O. of 11th Royal Scots at Stanmer.	
	30		Battalion Sports of the S/a 11th Royal Scots at Stanmer	

Army Form C. 2118.

WAR DIARY for July 1919
or
INTELLIGENCE SUMMARY.
(Erase heading not required.)

Place	Date	Hour	Summary of Events and Information	Remarks and references to Appendices
Title. Rhineland Germany Sheet 3. R.M.W. 1.25000 K.6704			Reinforcements	

J.R. Cobb
Captain
for Brigadier General
Commanding
2nd Lowland Brigade

War Diary

SECRET.
Copy No.....

2ND LOWLAND BRIGADE ORDER NO.6.

Reference Sheet 59, 1/250000.

1. The Lowland Division is replacing the Light Division in the IVth Corps.

2. The 2nd Lowland Brigade will be relieved by the 2nd Light Brigade. Relief to be completed by 19.00 hours, July 9th.

3. The 6th K.O.S.B. and 11th Royal Scots will be relieved on the Perimeter by the 9th London Regiment and 12th Royal Irish Rifles respectively.
    An advance party of two Companies, 2nd Light Brigade, who will take over the perimeter Posts, will arrive by lorry at 2nd Lowland Brigade H.Q. at 16.00 hours on the 8th. These two Companies will also relieve the Station Control and Railhead Guard at OHLIGS Station. Os.C., 6th K.O.S.B. and 11th Royal Scots will detail one guide per Post and one per Company H.Q. to report at 2nd Lowland Brigade H.Q. at 15.00 hours on the 8th.
    The Officer commanding Railway Control Post, OHLIGS Station will detail a guide to report 2nd Lowland Brigade H.Q. at same hour.
    The 5/6th Royal Scots will be relieved by the 6th London Regiment.
    The 2nd Lowland Brigade Group will entrain at OHLIGS Station in accordance with the attached Table. Echelon "B" Transport will proceed by march route. Orders will be issued later.

4. All details of relief will be arranged between Battalion Commanders concerned. All maps, Defence Schemes, details of Civil Administration, training facilities, educational instructions and recreational areas, Duties and Regulations of Perimeter Posts, Post S.A.A. and all requisitioned stores will be handed over on relief, and receipts received.

5. Civil Administration Staff of 2nd Lowland Brigade will remain in their present Area with the 2nd Light Brigade for one week.
    Civil Staff Captain of the 2nd Light Brigade will move with that Brigade.
    The personnel to be left behind will be as follows :-

    Staff Captain, C.A. & 2 Clerks.
    Provost Officer & 2 Clerks.
    KLUSE Post, 1 N.C.O. & 1 man.
    LOOP Post, 1 N.C.O. & 1 man.
    OHLIGS Railway Post, 2 Officers, 1 Sgt. & 4 men.

    This party at the end of a week will rejoin the Brigade Group under orders of the Staff Captain, Civil Administration.

    All other personnel will rejoin their Battalions on relief.

6. Progress and completion of moves and reliefs will be reported by wire to Brigade H.Q.

7. 2nd Lowland Brigade H.Q. will close at OHLIGS at 12.00 hours on July 9th., and will open at GILL at the same hour.
    2nd Lowland Brigade will on arrival in Light Divisional Area come under the command of the Light Division until 12.00 hours, July 10th.

8. ACKNOWLEDGE.

Distribution:- (Overleaf)

Captain,
Brigade Major,
2nd Lowland Brigade.

DISTRIBUTION.

Copy No. 1 to 5/6th Royal Scots.
        2 " 11th Royal Scots.
        3 " 6th K.O.S.B.
        4 " 2nd Lowland T.M.B.
        5 " 2nd Lowland Bde. School.
       6& 7 to 51st Bde. R.F.A.
       8 &9 " Lowland Bn. M.G.C.
      10 to 27th Field Ambulance.
      11 to 106th Coy. R.A.S.C.
      12 " 90th Fd. Coy. R.E.
      13 " G.O.C.
      14 " Brigade Major.
      15 " Staff Captain.
      16 " Staff Captain, Civil Admin.
      17 " Education Officer.
      18 " Bde. Signal Officer.
      19 " Intelligence Officer.
      20 " Bde. Transport Officer.
      21 " Lowland Divl. Train.
      22 " D.A.P.M., Lowland Division.
      23 " Brigade Provost Officer.
      24 " Lowland Division "G".
      25 "   "   "   "Q".
      26 " 2nd Light Brigade.
      27 " 1st Lowland Brigade.
      28 " 3rd   "   "
      29 " 16th H.L.I.(Pioneers).
      30 " Officer i/c Control Post, OHLIGS Stn.
      31 & 32. War Diary.
      33   File.

Issued through Signals
at *1800* hours, 7th July, 1919.

SECRET.

Copy No......

ADDENDUM NO.   TO 2ND LOWLAND BRIGADE ORDER NO.6.
===

Para. 5 of 2nd Lowland Brigade Order No.6 is cancelled, and the
following substituted :-

" The Civil Administrative Staff and personnel of the
2nd Lowland Brigade will remain in their present area
and will not be relieved by 2nd Light Brigade.
   The Staff and personnel to be left behind will be
as follows :-

   Staff Captain, Civil Duties & Clerks.
   Provost Officer & Clerks.
   KLUSE & LOOP Posts, Tramway Control personnel as
                                 at present.
   Summary Court Officer.
   Staff and personnel of OHLIGS Railway Control Post.

This personnel will probably be withdrawn within a
fortnight. "

MOVE OF 'B' ECHELON TRANSPORT.

'B' Echelon Transport of the Brigade Group as laid down in
Amendment to Administrative Orders accompanying 2nd Lowland Bde.
Order No.6 will proceed by march route to the new area under the
Brigade Transport Officer in accordance with March Table below.
   'B' Echelon will cross the Rhine by the Ferry at BENRATH
near to RHEININAN Oilworks. The crossing will be made in two
trips. The first at 08.00 hours and the second at 10.00 hours
on the 9th July.
   The Echelon will stage for the night of the 9th/10th at
DELRATH, and will march from there under orders to be issued by
the Brigade Transport Officer so as to reach Units by 12.00 hours
on the 10th.

MARCH TABLE FOR 'B' ECHELON TRANSPORT./

- 2 -.

MARCH TABLE FOR 'B' ECHELON TRANSPORT.

Serial No.	Unit.	Starting Point.	Time to pass S.P.	Route.	Remarks.
1.	27th Fd. Ambulance.	Where the OHLIGS - HAAN Railway crosses the WALD-HILDEN Road. K.8957.	05.15	HILDEN-BENRATH.	
	5/6th Royal Scots.	- do. -	05.20	do.	
	6th K.O.S.B.	- do. -	05.25	do.	
	11th Royal Scots.	Where the HAAN-HILDEN Road joins the OHLIGS-HILDEN Road at K.4459.	06.30	do.	To move in rear of 6th K.O.S.B.

The Brigade Transport Officer will arrange with the Inland Water Transport Officer at the Ferry what vehicles will cross by the 1st and 2nd Trips.

Issued through Signals
at 11⁰⁰ Hours on 8/7/19.

Captain,
Brigade Major,
2nd Lowland Brigade.

DISTRIBUTION:- Copy to All Recipients of
2nd Lowland Brigade Order No.6.

B.M.3/1.
4/9/19.

Lowland Division 'A'.

Herewith War Diaries of this Brigade H.Q. and three Battalions of the Brigade, for the month of August, 1919.

Please acknowledge.

Brigadier-General,
Commanding 2nd Lowland Brigade.

REINFORCEMENTS.

5/6th. Royal Scots.   11th. Royal Scots.   6th. K.O.S.B.

6. Other Ranks.   11. Other Ranks.   2. Officers 15. O.R.

Army Form C. 2118.

WAR DIARY for August 1919
INTELLIGENCE SUMMARY
(Erase heading not required.)

Instructions regarding War Diaries and Intelligence Summaries are contained in F.S. Regs., Part II. and the Staff Manual respectively. Title pages will be prepared in manuscript.

Place	Date	Hour	Summary of Events and Information	Remarks and references to Appendices
Y Holz Straw	7.8.19		11th Royal Scots & advance parties of Bn proceed to Düren area	App I
DÜREN RHEINLAND	8.8.19		2nd Lowland Brigade ordered R.Y. to move to Düren area	
GERMANY	14.8.19		Move to Düren	
	15.8.19		A.C.C. units in Düren that 90th R.E. (in Stockheim)	
	18.6.19		Tattoo, Torchlight demonstration at Niederggen	
	19.8.19		Brigade Commander inspected Bn H.Q. and Transport	
	20.8.19		O.I.C. inspected 11th Regt Scots	
	21.8.19		do 5/6 do do	
			O.I.C. inspected I.M.B.	
	22.8.19		2nd & 6 manoeuvres inspected Barracks	
	29.8.19		6th K.O.S.B. inspected by O.I.C.	
			C. Offy of Düren Defence Scheme (amended) issued to Battalion	
			Reinforcements	

C. Anderson
Lieut.
For Brigade Major
2nd Lowland Brigade

War Diary

2ND LOWLAND BRIGADE ORDER NO. 7.

SECRET.

Copy No......

Reference Sheet 59. 1/200000.

1.   The 2nd Lowland Brigade Group (less 11th Royal Scots now at DUREN) will move on the 14th and 15th inst. in accordance with attached March Table 'A'.

2.   The Brigade Group (less 106th Coy. R.A.S.C.) will move by lorry. Lorries are allotted and will report to Units as under.
     106th Coy. R.A.S.C. will move by road on 14th under orders of O.C., Company, to HINDENBURG Barracks, DUREN.

Date.	Unit.	No. of personnel to be carried by Lorries.	Extra Lorries for Stores.	Place of reporting.	Time.	Remarks.
14th.	2nd Lowland Bde. H.Q.	150.	3	GILL	09.00	
	6th K.O.S.B.	430.	12	Entrance to NIEDER-AUSSEM from BERGHEIM.	09.00	
	90th Fd.Coy. R.E.	100.	5*	VANIKUM.	09.00	3*lorries for drawing pontoons.
15th.	5/6th R.SCOTS.	650.	15	Entrance to BUTZHEIM on main ROMMERS/ KIRCHEN Road.	09.00	
	T.M.B.	42	2	BUSDORF.	09.00	

3.   Lorries for the conveyance of extra stores will be at the disposal of Os.C., Units, and will proceed under their orders. They must, however, travel by the route followed by Unit personnel lorries. Their movements must be so timed so as not to interfere with the movement of personnel columns.

4.   One lorry of each Battalion personnel column may, if necessary, be left behind to convey the loading party of the extra "store" lorries.

5.   Battn. extra "store" lorries will not move between the old and new areas in columns of less than 6 vehicles.

6./

- 2 -

6. Horse Transport will move by road under orders of Os.C Units. It will proceed via BERGHEIM-ELSDORF-BUIR-GOLZHEIM, and must be clear of the ELSDORF road junction before 11.00 hours each day.

7. 5/6th Royal Scots will leave a guard of 1 N.C.O. and 4 O.R. on the Ordnance Dump at ROMMERSKIRCHEN Jam Factory. They will be rationed up to and including 17th ; Lowland Division are making arrangements to ration them from 18th onwards, which will be notified later.

8. 28th Field Ambulance moved to DUREN to-day and will arrange the collection and evacuation of sick on arrival of Units.

9. 2nd Lowland Brigade H.Q. will close at GILL at 11.00 hours on 14th and open at DUREN at the same hour.

10. Completion of moves will be reported to Brigade H.Q.

11. Units of Brigade Group to acknowledge.

Captain,
Brigade Major,
2nd Lowland Brigade.

Issued through Signals
at 0830 hours.
13th August, 1919.

DISTRIBUTION.

No.1.	5/6th Royal Scots.	Nos. 12 & 13.		War Diary.
No.2.	11th Royal Scots.	No. 14.		G.O.C.
No. 3.	6th K.O.S.B.	No. 15.		B.M.
No. 4.	2nd Lowland T.M.B.	No. 16.		S.C.
No. 5.	90th Fd. Coy. R.E.	No. 17.		S.C., Civil Admin.
No. 6.	103th Coy. R.A.S.C.	No. 18.		Brigade Signal Officer
No. 7.	28th Fd. Ambulance.	No. 19.		" Transport Offr.
No. 8.	Lowland Div. "G".	No. 20.		" Provost Offr.
No. 9.	do. "Q".	No. 21.		File.
No.10.	1st Lowland Bde.			
No.11.	3rd do.			

2nd Lowland Brigade Order No. ?

Serial No.	Date.	Unit.	From.	To.	Starting Point.	Time.	Route.	Remarks.
1.	14th	2nd Lowland Brigade H.Q.	GILL	DUREN	The road junction at N in HOHENHOVEN.	11.00.	BERGHEIM. STEINSTRASSE. OBERZIER. MERKEN.	
2.	"	6th K.O.S.B.	NIEDER-AUSSEM	Billets DUREN.	The road junction just N. of the '3' in BERGHEIM.	11.15.	-do.-	
3.	"	90th Fd. Coy. R.E.	VANIKUM.	STOCKHEIM.	Eastern outskirts of VANIKUM.	11.15	ROMERSKIRCHEN RD. AUSSEM. BERGHEIM. STEINSTRASSE. OBERZIER. MERKEN.	
4.	15th	5/6th Royal Scots.	NETTESHEIM Area	HINDENBURG Barracks, DUREN.	Where the DORMAGEN-BERGHEIM Road crosses the ROMERSKIRCHEN-COLOGNE road.	10.00.	BERGHEIM. STEINSTRASSE. OBERZIER. MERKEN.	
5.	"	2nd Lowland T.M.B.	BUSDORF.	-do.-	BUSDORF Church.	11.00.	-do.-	

2nd. Lowland Brigade Reinforcements
September, 1919.

	Officers	Other Ranks.
5/6th. Royal Scots.	-	12.
11th. Royal Scots.	-	15.
8th. K.O.S.B.	-	-

Army Form C. 2118.

WAR DIARY for September 1919
or INTELLIGENCE SUMMARY.
(Erase heading not required.)

Place	Date	Hour	Summary of Events and Information	Remarks and references to Appendices
Holy Mount Dupin	15.9.19		4th Corps Headquarters disbanded. 2nd Lowland Brigade transferred to II Corps.	
Rheinland				
Germany	17.9.19		5/6th Royal Scots represent 4 Corps in athletic Events in Rhine Army Championship	
	21.9.19		Inspection by Divisional Commander of 6th R.O.S.B.	
	22.9.19		Congratulations General of Lowson Lewis departs to United Kingdom on leave. Lt Col Maclure D.S.O. 5/6 R. Scots Assumes command of Brigade	
	23.9.19		Divisional Scheme of forming reduction of Battalion to two Companies	
	24.9.19		Personnel of 2nd Lowland T.M.B. returned to units	
	25.9.19		6th K.O.S.B. Leave for U.K.	
	30.9.19		R.E. Signal Personnel return to Division. 5/6th Royal Scots reduced to 2 Companies Reinforcements.	

Mawson
Lieut.
for Brigade Major
2nd Lowland Brigade.

SECRET. 2nd Lowland Brigade Operation
Order......No. 10.

O.C. Dormagen Guard.
Civil Administration, Dormagen.
51st H.L.I.

3rd November, 1919.

(1). The Company of 51st H.L.I. at DORMAGEN will be relieved of their guard duties on November 4th. The guard will leave at appointed time whether the Barracks are taken over by the French or not.

(2). They will leave by train (time to be notified later) for BEDBURG via COLOGNE.

(3) A lorry will report at 09-00 hours to convey baggage &c to BEDBURG. This may be kept for two journeys if necessary.

(4). All Requisitioned Barrack Stores will be handed over to the Burgmeister of the area and receipts will be obtained in duplicate and one copy forwarded to this office.

(5). St. Peters Post will also be withdrawn.

(6). Completion of relief will be wired to this Headquarters.

Captain,
Brigade Major,
2nd Lowland Brigade.

Copy to:-
File.
II Corps.
Staff Captain.

WAR DIARY
or
INTELLIGENCE SUMMARY

Army Form C. 2118.

Place	Date	Hour	Summary of Events and Information	Remarks and references to Appendices
DUREN	1/10/19	—	Nothing to report	
	2 "	—	do	
	3 "	—	do	
	4 "	—	do	
	5 "	—	do	
	6 "	—	do	
	7 "	—	do	
	8 "	—	do	
	9 "	—	do	
	10 "	—	do	
	11 "	—	do	
	12 "	—	do	
	13 "	—	do	
	14 "	—	15th Bn. H.L.I. came to DUREN, and came under Command of G.O.C. 2nd Lowland Bde.	
	15 "	—	Nothing to report	
	16 "	—	do	
	17 "	—	do	
	18 "	—	Divn. Defence Scheme (Amended) issued to all Units.	
	19 "	—	Nothing to report	
	20 "	—	do	
	21 "	—	do	
	22 "	—	do	
	23rd "	—	Divn. H.Q. disbanded 12.0 hours. All remaining Divnl. Units came under Command of G.O.C. 2nd Lowland Bde.	
	24th "	—	S/o returned to Cadre. All returnable personal Transferred to 11th	
	25 M	—	5/6th Royal Scots. Royal Scots.	

Sheet 2

WAR DIARY
or
INTELLIGENCE SUMMARY.

Army Form C. 2118.

(Erase heading not required.)

Place	Date	Hour	Summary of Events and Information	Remarks and references to Appendices
DUREN	26/10/19	—	Nothing to report	
	27/10/19	—	Capt. G.B. GROOM, M.C., Brigade Major left to return to War Office. Capt. S.J. GOUGH, M.C., G.S.O.3 Lowland Div. assumed duties.	
	28/10/19	—	Nothing to report	
	29/10/19	—	do	
	30/10/19	—	2nd Lowland Bde. Defence Scheme issued to all Units of Bde. and Divl. Details	
	31/10/19	—	Nothing to report	

Gough Capt.
Bde. Major
2nd Lowland Bde.

SECRET.

Copy No............ 22

B.M./2//D.S. 30/10/18.

II Corps.
VI Corps.
11th. Royal Scots.
16th. H.L.I.
51st. H.L.I.
50th. Bde. R.F.A.
51st. Bde. R.F.A.
C.R.E.
9th. M.G.C.
77th. French Division.
Lowland Divl., Train.
D.A.P.M. DUREN
Civil Administration DUREN.
H.Q., Tank Group.
92nd. Siege Battery, R.G.A.
A.D.M.S.
Officer i/c Barracks.
Lowland Divl., M.T. Coy.
G.O.C.
Brigade Major.
Staff-Captain.
File.

Herewith now complete DEFENCE SCHEME for whole of 2nd Lowland Brigade Area.

Please acknowledge on form below.

[signed] H. Gough
Captain,
Brigade Major,
2nd Lowland Brigade.

Received Copy No............ 2nd Lowland Brigade DEFENCE SCHEME.

....

....

SECRET.

2ND LOWLAND BRIGADE DEFENCE SCHEME.

Copy No,

Reference Map 1.K., 2.K., and 1.L. 1/100,000.

1. Responsibility in Civil Disturbances.

    (a) Every Commander is responsible for preparing and keeping up to date a scheme for the employment of all troops under his command in the event of civil disturbances.

    (b) In each scheme provision should be made for some formed body of troops to be at the disposal of the Commander for employment anywhere within the area for which he is responsible, or for reinforcing a neighbouring area in case of necessity.

    (c) A map showing the sub-division of the 2nd Lowland Brigade Area is attached.

    (d) Commanders are responsible for dealing with all disturbances within their areas.

2. General Principles.

    Defence Schemes will be framed in accordance with the following principles :-

    (a) **Provision for the safe guarding of Government property and establishments.**

    (b) Provision for the protection of certain vulnerable points (See para. 3).

    (c) Retention of a mobile reserve.

3. Upkeep of Local Defence Schemes.

    Local Defence Schemes will be kept up to date in tabular form by the Commanders of Sub-Areas. (Specimen attached Appendix 'A').

    There will be three Sub-Areas :-

    (a) DUREN.
    (b) BEDBURG, (including DORMAGEN until taken over by French).
    (c) ELSDORF.

    These schemes will be kept constantly under review during the process of reduction and re-organization, modifications being made as necessity arises.

The vulnerable ....

- 2 -

3. (Continued).

The vulnerable points referred to in Para 2 (b) are as follows:-

DUREN Area.

(1) Sheet 1.L., J.5.   DUREN WATER SUPPLY.
    73-70

(2) Sheet 1.L., H.5.   Viaduct at Kilo. 48.3. 4 spans of 4 M.
    99-80   2 of 3.5 M. 1 of 9.5 M. Brick Arches
                          carrying Railway over Road & Stream.

(3) Sheet 1.L., J.5.   Kilo. 40.6.   Bridge, 5 spans
    50 - 47.   of 11.5 M. Brick Arches carrying
                          Railway over River ROER.

(4) Sheet 1.L., J.5.   Kilo. 39.6. Bridge 5 spans of 4.3.M.
    65 - 67.   Brick Arches carrying Railway over
                          Road.

(5) Sheet 1.L., J.5.   Kilo. 39.3. Bridge 3 spans of 5 M.
    70 - 62   Concrete Arch & Steel girder, carrying
                          Railway over Road and footway.

BEDBURG Area.

Sheet 1.L. M.1.   (1) FORTUNA ELECTRIC POWER STATION.
65.20   (Nr. BERGHEIM).

Sheet 1.L. O.10. (2) FACTORY at DORMAGEN.

ELSDORF Area.

(1) Sheet 1.L. M.3.   Kilo. 20.2. Bridge, 2 spans of 8.M. Brick
    84 - 98   Arches carrying Railway over River ERFT.

(2) Sheet 1.L. M.2.   Kilo. 20.0 Bridge 2 spans of 8 M. Brick
    89 - 01.   Arch carrying Railway over Canal.

(3) Sheet 1.L. M.2.   Kilo. 19.5. Bridge 2 spans of 8 M. Brick
    97 - 07.   Arch carrying Railway over Road and Stream.

N.B. These vulnerable points are in addition to those already enumerated in the present Defence Scheme for DUREN Area.

4. Co-operation of R.A.F.

Arrangements have been made with No. 12 Squadron R.A.F., to co-operate with Corps, Divisions and Brigades, in the event of Civil disturbances of a serious nature in the Corps Area.

The Squadron will be prepared to carry out a reconnaissance of any part of the Corps Area, and to drop reports at Corps, Division, or Brigade Headquarters.

5. **Code Words and Action Required.**

   (A) In the event of a serious disturbance being apprehended the following Code Words will be sent out by Brigade Hdqrs.

   Warning Order — DUBLIN.

   Order to Move — BELFAST

   On receipt of the Code Word DUBLIN.

   (a) All troops will be held in readiness to move at 1 hour's notice.

   On receipt of Code word BELFAST.

   (a) All troops, except those in reserve, will proceed at once to the stations allotted to them in their local Defence Schemes.

   (B) In the event of a local disturbance the Commander on the spot will take such action to quell it as he considers necessary, bearing in mind that judicious action in the first instance will frequently nip the trouble in the bud and prevent it growing to serious dimensions.

6. **The Alarm.**

   All Local Defence Schemes will include arrangements for sounding the Alarm, whether by bugles, hooters or other means, and will lay down the action of the troops when the Alarm is sounded.

7. **General Instructions to Commanders in dealing with Civil Disturbances.**

   It is not possible to frame instructions applicable to all circumstances, and the employment of force in Civil disturbances must be left largely to the discretion of the Commander on the spot.

   The principle to bear in mind is that the employment of force should be strictly limited to what is required in order to obtain the desired object.

   The following instructions may be taken as a guide to officers in command of parties employed on such duty :-

   (i) No large crowd will be allowed to collect in the vicinity of troops or of Military Establishments.

   (ii) Civilians carrying arms will be arrested.

   (iii) Civilians making use of firearms or explosives will be shot. Looting, damage to property or communications and acts of incendiarism will be prevented, by shooting if necessary.

7. General Instructions to Commanders in dealing with civil disturbances. (contd.)

   (iv) Fire on crowds will not be opened unless they assume a threatening attitude, and then only by order of the senior officer on the spot.

   (v) Fire, when opened, must be effective. Firing over the heads of a crowd with a view to intimidating them is absolutely forbidden.

8. Flying column.

   Each Area Commander should keep a "Flying Column" at his disposal, ready to move by lorry, or improvised transport at very short notice to any locality where such a disturbance might arise.

9. Attached are:-

   (1) Appendix "A" Local Defence Scheme of DUREN.
   (2)   do.   "B"   "   "   "   " BEDBURG.
   (3)   do.   "C"   "   "   "   " ELSDORF.
   (4)   do.   "D" Map of Area.

                                    Captain,
                                    Bde. Major,
                                    2nd Lowland Brigade.

DEFENCE SCHEME FOR CIVIL DISTURBANCES.

DÜREN.

Officer in Command, O.C., 11th Royal Scots.

HINDENBURG BARRACKS.

Troops Available.	Approx. Strength.	Alarm Post.	Alarm Signal.	Points to be Guarded.	Strength.	Found by.
11th Bn. R.SCOTS. 15th H.L.I. 108th Coy. A.S.C. 5 Fd. Coys. R.E. 92nd Siege Bty. R.G.A. 'D' Area Sig. Coy. 55th Sanitary Sect. Low. Div. M.T. Coy.	2200.	HINDENBURG Barracks. do. Billets. NORD SCHUL. Telegraph Office. 12, ESCH Str. Sugar Factory PARADIES STR.	(1) SYRENS from RATHAUS -swelling sounds of 2 minutes duration. (2) Jodo Works by 'phone DUBLIN & BELFAST. (3) BUGLES.	(1) DUREN WATER SUPPLY. L.L. J.5. 72-70.	1 Platoon,	11th Royal Scots.
				(2) VIADUCT. L.L. H.5. 99-80	1 platoon.	15th H.L.I.
				(3) BRIDGE. L.L.u.5. 50-47. (4) BRIDGE. M.L.J.5. 65-57. (5) BRIDGE. L.M.J.5. 70-62. (6) RAILWAY STATION	Headquarters & Reserve.	11th Royal Scots. 11th Royal Scots. 11th Royal Scots.
				(7) H.Q. Offices. (6) Offices, ESSENBAHN STR.	Military Police & H.Q. Clerks. 1 Platoon	Guard on duty reinforced to 1 Platoon by 11th Royal Scots.
				(9) WATER TOWER, COLN PLATZ. (10) POST & TELEGRAPH OFFICES.	1 Platoon.	11th R. SCOTS. 'D' Area Sig. Coy. & Sig.At Railway Stn.
				(11) BIERBRAUEREI at ARNOLDSWEILER STRASSE.	Corps Sup. Coy. & Ordnance Working Party.	
				(12) DIV. Reception Camp. (13) NORD SCHULE.		Labour Coy. Cadre 92nd Siege Bty. R.G.A.
				(14) RATHAUS. (15) PARADIES STR. (16) PESCH SCHULE (Inlying Picquet)	1 platoon. 1 platoon. 1 Coy. less 1 platoon.	11th R. SCOTS. Div. M.T. Coy. 11th R. SCOTS.

Appendix 1.

Patrols.	Found By.	Reserves.	Where assembled.	Remarks.
		15th H.L.I. and all remaining troops.	HINDENBURG BARRACKS.	

APPENDIX "3".

DEFENCE SCHEME FOR CIVIL DISTURBANCES.

51st H.L.I.

Officer in Command......Lt.Col. SEGRAVE, D.S.O. Bedburg.

Troops available.	Approx. Strength.	Alarm Post.	Alarm Signal.	Points to be guarded.	Strength.	Found by.	Reserves.	Where assembled.
51st H.L.I.	650.	Barrack Square, Schloss, Bedburg.	Bugle.	(a) Fortuna Power Station.	2 platoons.	51st H.L.I.	Remainder of 51st H.L.I.	Barrack Square, Schloss, BEDBURG.
				(b) DORMAGEN Factory.	1 coy.(now at this station.	do.		
				(c) Burgmeister's house & office.	2 sections.	do.		
				(d) 51st Q.M.Stores.	2 sections.	do.		
				(e) Post & Telegraph Office.	2 sections.	do.		

APPENDIX "B".

Defence Scheme. BEDBURG SUB-AREA.

(1) In the event of civil disturbances in this area, it is the intention of the Sub-area Commandant to keep the troops concentrated as far as possible with the object of taking action in strength against the main centre of disturbance.

(2) On receipt of information that disturbances are likely to occur, the battalion buglers will sound the alarm in different quarters of BEDBURG; and all troops will be confined to barracks - in the Schloss, BEDBURG. Messengers will be despatched to DORMAGEN and outlying detachments.

(3) Guards and detachments will be posted at vulnerable points as shown below:-

Fortuna Works.	2 Platoons.
Dormagen Factory.	1 coy. (now at this station.)
Burgomaster's House and Office.	2 Sections.
Q.M.Stores, Bedburg.	2 Sections.
Post & Teleg. Office.	2 Sections.

These with the exception of DORMAGEN will be found by the company on duty.

(4) Troops will wear fighting order with 60 rounds S.A.A. per man.

SECRET.   Defence Scheme for Civil Disturbances – ELSDORF Area.   APPENDIX "C".
                           Officer in Command – Lieut. Colonel A.K.R. MALLOCK, R.F.A.
                           Commanding 50th Brigade R.F.A.

Troops available.	Approx. Strength.	Alarm Post.	Alarm Signal.	Telephone.	Points to be guarded.	Strength.	Found by.	Supports.	Reserve.	Where assembled.
50th Brigade RFA.	200 Rifles.	ELSDORF HUTS. Billets.		Mounted Orderly.	Railway Bridges. Sheet. 1L N5 8498. 1G M2 8901.	1 N.C.O. 12 men 1 Lewis Gun.	A/50 RFA.	Remainder A/50.		SINDORF.
51st Brigade RFA.	16 Lewis Guns.	Billets.			Sheet 1L M2 9707 Railway Signal Box Sheet 1L N2 1013	1 N.C.O. 12 men 1 Lewis Gun	C/50. RFA.	Remainder C/50	All Remaining Troops.	Billets.
	32 Guns.					Lt. Wheeler A/50 in charge.				
					Battery Headquarters.		Batteries concerned.			

On warning of disturbance, A/50 RFA and C/50 RFA will at once send forward armed picquet as per schedule in G.S. Wagons,
and guard points mentioned.
These Batteries will move forward in support to SINDORF as soon as possible.

The remaining batteries of the 50th and 51st Brigades will be prepared to move at an hour's notice.
All men armed with rifles will be served out with 60 rounds of ammunition, and will be held in immediate readiness.
All Lewis Guns will be ready for immediate use with full complement of ammunition.
Reports to 50th Brigade H.Q., NIEDEREMBT.

SECRET.

BM/5/D.S.
18th October, 1919.

5/6th Royal Scots.
11th Royal Scots.
15th H.L.I.
106th Coy. R.A.S.C.
O.C., Fd. Coys R.E.
D.A.P.M., DUREN.
Staff Captain, Civil Admin, DUREN.
92nd. Siege Bty. R.G.A.
H.Q. Tank Group.
'D' Area Signal Coy.
53rd Sanitary Section.
Camp Commandant, IV Corps.
28th Fd. Ambulance.
O.C., 11th. Stationary Hosp.
O.C., 2nd Corps Troops.
Officer, i/c Barracks.
Lowland Div. M.T. Coy.
O.C., Divn. Train.
G.O.C.,
Brigade Major.
Staff Captain,
Lowland Division.

       Herewith Copy No .... DUREN DEFENCE SCHEME (Amended).

       The Amended Scheme will come into force on 19th October, 1919.

       All previous DEFENCE SCHEMES will be destroyed.

       Acknowledge on form below.

                                    C.Anderson Lt.,
                               for Brigade Major,
                         2nd Lowland Brigade.

Received Copy No......... DUREN DEFENCE SCHEME.

DUREN DEFENCE SCHEME.
(Amended).

Copy No..............

1. General Object.

The following arrangements have been drawn up with a view to maintaining order in the Town and outskirts of DUREN in the event of a riot or local disturbance being caused by the civil population.

2. Responsibility.

Any disturbance which is not of a serious nature will be dealt with by the D.A.P.M. assisted by his Police, supported by "Inlying Picquet" (See Para. 9), which is placed at his disposal for this purpose.

3. Procedure in the Event of a Riot or Serious Disturbance.

Should a riot or serious disturbance arise, in any quarter of the Town, the G.O.C., 2nd Lowland Brigade will at once be informed of its locality and nature. Should military precautions be deemed necessary, the D.A.P.M. will order the "ALARM" (swelling sounds of 2 minutes duration) to be sounded on the syrens from the RATHHAUS (See Appendix 2) and will send by telegraph or other means the word "RIOT" to the G.O.C., 2nd Lowland Brigade.

As an alternative means to the syren, the D.A.P.M. will warn the nearest guard to sound the "ALARM" on the bugles. This will be taken up by all Guards within hearing.

4. Action by the Civil Population.

The local Authorities have been informed that immediately the syrens sound the "ALARM" all civilians have to quit the streets.

5. Action by the Troops.

(a) On the syrens or bugles sounding the "ALARM", all troops, as detailed in para. 7 will at once "STAND TO" and prepare to move to their allotted stations.

(b) Any other troops in DUREN will at once proceed to the RAMP leading to the Station, where they will be organized into parties by an Officer who has been specially detailed for this purpose.

6. Policy which will be adopted when troops have taken up their allotted Posts.

(a) Certain selected localities will be held, and the town energetically patrolled. (The location, strength, and name of Units generally responsible for holding these posts is contained in Appendix 1).

(b) No civilians will be allowed to move about the streets. This will prevent parties of rioters moving from one locality to another.

(c) Os.C., Battalions will ensure that Posts allotted to them are thoroughly reconnoitred by the Officers who have to take charge of them, that sites for Lewis Guns are carefully chosen with a view to covering all the approaches of the posts, and that communication between the posts and Battalion Headquarters, by runner, can be maintained at all times.

(d) ....

- 2 -

(d) Troops will carry 80 rounds of S.A.A. per man.
Lewis Guns with 8 drums per gun will be manhandled to the posts.

(e) Troops will not fire unless :-

    (1) Rioters adopt a menacing attitude.
    (2) Attempt to force the posts.
    (3) Looting or destruction of shops or houses is being resorted to.

NOTE. A few rounds fired by Lewis Guns or rifles in any of the above cases would most probably nip in the bud a disturbance which might otherwise assume serious proportions and lead to much bloodshed.

(f) The Os.C. Areas will utilise their reserve in patrolling and taking energetic action to disperse crowds, etc., etc.

(g) All civilians with arms in their hands will be at once shot or captured.

(h) Ringleaders will be arrested and confined in a house near where the post is situated. No attempt will be made till the disturbance has subsided, to hand these ringleaders over to the Sub-Area Commandant, as this might entail attempts to rescue them.

7. Disposition of Troops during "ALARM" Period.

The town of DUREN is divided into two Battalion Areas. The Os.C., Battalions will command all Troops billeted in their Areas and will be responsible for maintaining order in their areas. A mobile reserve will be kept at the Barracks. (Localities to be defended, see Appendix 1).

DUREN - West Area.

Town west of VELDENER STRASSE, EISENBAHN STRASSE, South of the Railway WIRTEL STRASSE, OBER STRASSE.

DUREN - East Area.

East of above named streets.

DUREN - East Area.

Commander : O.C., 'A' Bn., 2nd Lowland Brigade.

Troops : 'A' Bn. 2nd Lowland Brigade.

Headquarters : Railway Station.

DUREN - WEST Area.

Commander : O.C., 'B' Bn. 2nd Lowland Brigade.

Troops : 'B' Bn. and Inlying Picquet.

Headquarters : H.Q., Inlying Picquet at SCHULE.

Reserve........

- 3 -

Reserve.

   Commander : O.C., 'C' Bn. 2nd Lowland Brigade.

   Troops : 'C' Bn.

Barracks.

   Commander : O.C., Field Coys. R.E.

   Troops : Details 'A', 'B', and 'C' Battalions, R.E., and R.A.S.C.

8. Sounding of the "All Clear".

As soon as he considers that the disturbance has been quelled the G.O.C, 2nd Lowland Brigade will give the order for the "ALL CLEAR" to be sounded, i.e. a succession of short blasts of the syren.

9. Inlying Picquet.

One Company of Infantry will be billeted in the SCHULE in the centre of the Town and will act as INLYING PICQUET. One platoon will always be available to turn out at five minutes notice, and the remainder at half-an-hour after the sounding of the "ALARM" by the syren or bugles, or unless otherwise ordered.

It can be called upon direct by the D.A.P.M. to deal with any minor local disturbance or to support the Military Police, and the Company Headquarters will be connected to his office by a direct telephone line.

The D.A.P.M. will at once inform the G.O.C, 2nd Lowland Brigade should he call upon the INLYING PICQUET.

H.Q., 2nd Lowland Brigade.

18th October, 1919.

Captain,
Brigade Major,
2nd Lowland Brigade.

APPENDIX 1.

Localities to be defended.

DUREN - East Area.

Locality.	Garrison.
1. Railway Station.	Guard Battn. H.Q. and Reserve.
2. H.Q., Offices.	Military Police & Clerks.
3. Offices, EISENBAHN Str.	Guard reinforced to 1 platoon.
4. Water Tower, KOIN PLATZ.	1 Platoon.
5. Post & Telegraph Office.	'D' Area Signal Coy. & Light Railway Signal Coy.
6. Bierbrauerei, ARNOLDSWEILER STR.	Corps Employment Coy. & Ordnance Working parties.
7. Junction ZULPICHER Str. & NIDEGGENER STR.	1 Platoon.
8. NORD SCHULE.	Cadre, 92nd Siege Battery, R.G.A. plus Dump Guard.
9. Divl. Reception Camp.	Det. Labour Corps and men billeted there.

DUREN - WEST AREA.

Locality.	Garrison.
1. RATHHAUS.	1 platoon Inlying Picquet reinforced by remaining 3 platoons when relieved at SCHULE by H.Q. 'B' Bn. and 2 Companies.
2. Inlying Picquet H.Q., SCHULE.	H.Q., 'B' Bn. and 2 Companies.
3. PARADIES Str.	Div. M.T. Coy.
4. Opera House.	2 Companies.
5. Brigade H.Q. Mess.	Brigade H.Q. Servants.

APPENDIX 2.

Signal for alarming the Town.

The following is a translation of a notice which has appeared in the local newspapers :-

" The British Military Authorities, in order to clear the streets of all people for any reason whatsoever, will forthwith use the Alarm Syrens which formerly were worked by the Town Municipality with the view to advising the inhabitants of air raids. With regard to the Alarm, the Sub-Area Commandant of DUREN has issued the following orders :-

1. ALARM will be sounded in the same manner as was done when air raids were reported, i.e. by swelling sounds of 2 minutes duration.

2. As soon as the ALARM is sounded, all people walking in the streets must take refuge in the nearest house, and householders must give refuge to all entering their houses for safety.

3. The streets must be cleared at once by all civilians. Any one not under cover within five minutes is liable to be fired upon as a disturber of the peace.

4. "ALL CLEAR" will be given as formerly, after the danger is over, i.e. short sounds of 1 minute duration.

5. The signal will be tested every evening until further notice, i.e. short sounds of quarter minute duration, just in the same manner as formerly at 18.00 hours.

6. Alarms Signals are already installed in the following positions :-

    ST. ANNES CHURCH (1)
    ST. JOACHIMS CHURCH (1)   } Inside DUREN.
    OLD WATERWORKS (1)
    NEW WATERWORKS (1)

    ISOLA WORKS, BIRKESDORF (1)
    POWDER FACTORY, GURTZENICH (1) } Suburbs.

These are worked by one switch which is affixed at the Police Office, RATHHAUS, DUREN.

2nd Lowland Bde. H.Q. WAR DIARY for Month of November Army Form C. 2118.
or
INTELLIGENCE SUMMARY.

Place	Date	Hour	Summary of Events and Information	Remarks and references to Appendices
Duren	1/11/19	—	2nd Lowland Brigade Order No. 8 issued – Re taking over of Area by troops	Off. 1.
	2/11/19	—	" " " " No 9 issued – "	Off. 2
	3/11/19	—	" " " " No.10 issued – Re entrainment of 51st H.L.I.	Off. 3
	4/11/19	—	Nothing to report	
	5/11/19	—	11th Royal Scots and 15th H.L.I. move by train from DUREN to COLOGNE	
	6/11/19	—	51st H.L.I. entrain at BEDBURG, in deme't. stock to U.K. 2nd Lowland Bde. H.Q. disbanded 12.00 hours. Lowland Bde. took over Lowland Division Area	

Capt.
Brigade Major
2nd Lowland Brigade.

Secret.   Copy no......

2nd Lowland Brigade Order No. 9.

1. The area comprising the Kreises of DUREN, EUSKIRCHEN, RHEINBACH, MONTJOIE and SCHLEIDEN will be handed over to the French on 6th November.

2. With the exception of the necessary guards over material, all British Troops, other than Tank Corps personnel now in the above areas will be withdrawn.

2. The 15th H.L.I. will find all guards which are to be left, (a complete list will be sent later) from, as far as possible, men who are volunteers for the Army of the Rhine. These will mount on Nov. 4th and will be rationed by arrangements to be made by II Corps. Officer will be left in charge of the guards. These will rejoin the Battalion on completion of guard duties.

3. Orders for 50th and 51st Bdes. R.F.A. to move into Southern Divl. Area have already been issued.

4. The 15th H.L.I. will move by train on November 5th to RIEHL Barracks and will come under the orders of VI Corps.

5. The 51st H.L.I. will remain in its present locations, but will come under the orders of VI Corps at 10-00 hours on November 5th.

6. The 5/6th Royal Scots Cadre will move to Rhine Army Reception Camp on November 3rd by train from DUREN.

7. The Tank Group will remain at DUREN until further orders.

8. Orders as to disposal of material will be issued later.
All requisitioned stores, buildings, &c will be handed back to German authorities and receipts obtained.

9. The French will send advance parties to take over barracks &c on 4th Nov. Any troops remaining behind in the area to be handed over will come under the orders of the French on Nov. 6th.

10. Orders re 212th Employment Coy. will be issued later.

11. The picquet billet will be carefully cleaned and vacated on morning of Nov. 4th, the requisitioned stores being handed over to the German authorities and receipts obtained.
This school will be occupied by French troops.
All troops will move on Nov. 4th to the Barracks.

12. The range guard will be relieved by the French on Nov. 4th if possible.

13. The 11th Royal Scots will move to Cologne about Nov. 6th as a battalion prior to embarking for England, train arrangements will follow, approximate date of sailong for England November 14th.

14. Acknowledge by wire.

                                    Signed T.J.GOUGH,
                                        Captain,
                                        Brigade Major,
                                        2nd Lowland Brigade.

SECRET.   Copy No......

2nd LOWLAND BRIGADE ORDER No. 9.

Reference 2nd Lowland Brigade Order No. 8, para.2.

As the 15th H.L.I. will in all probability start for England on Nov. 7th they will be relieved of all guards mentioned in above paragraph.

These guards will be found by 11th Royal Scots.

The following are the guards necessary to be left behind:-

(1).   A.D.O.S. (Central Dump).
       No. 9 ARNOLDSWEILER STRASSE.

(2).   No.11 Stationary Hospital,
       AUSTALT-ALTEJULICHER STRASSE.

These guards each consist of 2 N.C.Os. and 7 men (including 1 cook) and will mount on morning of Nov. 4th.

All other Guards and Fatigue Parties distributed in this area will be withdrawn at NOON of Nov. 4th.

The Railhead Guard at Duren Station will be relieved by a stick guard of Labour Coy. The present guard will leave at 14-00 hours, Nov. 4th.

Acknowledge.

                              Signed. T.G.GOUGH, Captain,
                                    Brigade Major,
                                      2nd Lowland Brigade.

www.ingramcontent.com/pod-product-compliance
Lightning Source LLC
Chambersburg PA
CBHW081439160426
43193CB00013B/2331